THE
HOP BIN

FRAN & GEOFF DOEL

THE
HOP BIN

*An Anthology of Hop Picking
in Kent and East Sussex*

The
History
Press

*To Anne Hughes in grateful acknowledgement of
her inspirational articles in this book and of her
extensive contributions to Kent local history.*

First published 2014

The History Press
The Mill, Brimscombe Port
Stroud, Gloucestershire, GL5 2QG
www.thehistorypress.co.uk

© Fran & Geoff Doel, 2014

The right of Fran & Geoff Doel to be identified as the Authors
of this work has been asserted in accordance with the
Copyright, Designs and Patents Act 1988.

British Library Cataloguing in Publication Data.
A catalogue record for this book is available from the British Library.

ISBN 978 0 7524 9361 9

Typesetting and origination by The History Press
Printed in Great Britain

CONTENTS

ACKNOWLEDGEMENTS

We are indebted to Anne Hughes who has generously allowed us to use substantial parts of her academic essay 'The Early Years of Hop Growing in Kent', her account of the hop pickers' memorial service in Hadlow in 2003 and for the use of Alice Ransom's letter with her account of the Hartlake Bridge Disaster.

For permission to quote the extracts from George Orwell's accounts of his hop-picking experiences we acknowledge the estate of the late Sonia Brownell Orwell and Martin Secker & Warburg Ltd.

Direct quotations from Vita Sackville-West's *Country Notes* are 'Copyright Vita Sackville-West'.

The extract from H.E. Bates's *The Blossoming World* is reproduced by kind permission of Laurence Pollinger Ltd.

We should also like to thank the following for their help and contributions: Gael and Oliver Nash, John Lander, Bob Brown, Bob Kenward and Ken Thompson, and also our publishing team at The History Press: Nicola Guy, Declan Flynn, Emily Locke and Lucy Simpkin for the illustration on page 35.

PREFACE

Today the words 'beer' and 'ale' are often used interchangeably but historically they are not the same beverage. Until the thirteenth century the predominant drink of Northern Europe and for all classes was spiced ale, brewed with malt. Brewed on a domestic scale, ale was cloudy, sweet and nutritious, but did not keep and did not travel well without spoiling. The addition of an extra ingredient into ale – the hop – not only changed the taste, making it bitter, it helped to preserve the concoction much longer and stabilised it. By 1400 this new flavoursome drink, now labelled 'bier' and later anglicised as 'beer', was being made on a commercial scale abroad and being imported into England, and proved so popular that by the 1440s surveyors of ale brewers in London were replaced by surveyors of beer brewers. It seems that skilled Flemings and the Dutch made the good-quality beer, but that some London brewers were attempting to brew hop beer (though not always successfully) and were consequently being fined for the results.

We are fortunate today that the Internet gives us ready access to archivist material as some of our earliest English accounts on the cultivation and management of the hop garden in Kent date to the Tudor period. By the late Tudor period very large tracts of farmland in Kent had been successfully converted into hop gardens, the Kentish soil being peculiarly suited to the cultivation of hops. These manuals tell us that what a hop farm also required was plenty of combustibles (initially wood later charcoal) needed to fire the kilns which would dry the hops, as well as designated areas of land dedicated to the growth of ash or alder wood which would be used for the supporting hop-poles. The hops were initially trained by the 'mound method', that is planted in a small earth mound in which were inserted three small poles to each hill. The cost of setting up a new hop garden was considerable, particularly as the farmer needed to employ a large labour force to harvest the hops in his hop fields during the short picking season. However, many of the Kent farmers could apparently afford the high initial outlay and, with good husbandry, were able apparently to make their fortune.

Initially the harvesting of the hop was done by a local workforce – later supplemented by workers from outside the area. The picking 'season' in Kent started in early September and the harvesting could continue over a six-week period. Rain was a disaster as no money could be earned and the crop lost. From the beginning, farmers encouraged married women to be an important part of the labour force, permitting them to bring their children into the fields and to help with the picking.

In the seventeenth century, hop cultivation in Kent had become so widespread and commercial and beer production had become so successful that the new breweries in Canterbury, Birchington, Dover, Deal, Hythe, Maidstone and Chatham were supplying overseas markets as well as local. And although hops were now grown in thirteen other counties, it was Kent that supplied one-third of all hop crops. The Long Parliament, then waging war against their king and desperate for revenue, capitalised on their success by imposing a beer tax in 1643 which initially also affected domestic brewers though the despised levy on domestic brewing was lifted in 1651. Ale houses as well as many of the wealthier households at this time were building their own brew houses so that they could produce their own beer.

The eighteenth century has a prolific amount of literary material on hopping which relates to the fact that beer had now firmly replaced ale in England as the most general drink for all classes and that the crop was now therefore both important economically and lucrative for the farmer; it also tells us that many farmers were literate and could afford to buy printed books on farm management. By the end of the century thousands of acres of farmland in Kent were dedicated to hop production, creating a distinctive landscape of fields in which lines of geometrically placed high poles sustained growing or trailing bines, the whole protected by windbreaks of trees and dotted by picturesque oast houses which housed the kilns to dry the hops.

In the Victorian period, journalists observed and wrote magazine articles about the Kentish hop gardens and their pickers for an interested middle-class public and these, as well as hopping songs and poems, give us an insight today into how the harvesting of the hop generated its own rituals and superstitions during this period. A number of scholars have pointed out that 'part of the mystique of the hop gardens' was that from Tudor times onwards hopping had a special language partly derived from its specialised tools including the 'hop dog', the 'hop peddler' and the 'hop spud'. Later in the Victorian period there would be other new words – the 'furiners' arriving in 'Hopping Specials', and the specially built 'Hoppers' Huts'. In addition to this the red neckchiefs adopted by the men gave them a jaunty European look and the exotic stilts worn by the Kentish men as they took giant strides through the hop garden must have generated some excitement, as did the arrival of the gaily painted Gypsy caravans in the early period. In the first half of the century the late Georgian and then the Victorian conscience was pricked by accounts of the yearly mass exodus by thousands of London's poorest 'in a ragged procession' as they made their way often on foot along the Old Kent Road to the hop fields of Kent. The union workhouses could supply some with overnight accommodation en route but there was little else provided for them when they arrived and it was often unhygienic, with farmers often proffering accommodation normally reserved for their animals – stables, cattle sheds, barns, even pigsties – to house the hopping families. Washing and toilet facilities were equally primitive at this time. Eventually farmers were inspired to provide shelter for them under canvas – early photos seem to indicate they used surplus ex-army tents made for some long-forgotten war. Purpose-built huts came last of all.

Bob Brown and family hop picking in the 1950s. (Courtesy of the late Bob Brown)

Machine picking began to displace hand picking during the 1950s and by the 1960s the 'furiners' workforce was simply no longer needed. And so, not with a bang but a whimper, ended the great exodus of East Enders from London to the hop fields along with the Gypsy and Irish 'tinkers' that joined them – all very much a thing of the past. The landscape itself changed as the hop fields and their hop poles disappeared one by one leaving oast houses isolated in the midst of great empty green fields. Nostalgia set in and the twentieth century saw, transcribed from taped interviews, lively accounts from farmers and pickers about their experiences in the hop gardens, now considered important socio-historical records. In folk clubs the old hopping songs were remembered, sung and recorded. New museums were created, often in old oast houses, celebrating the golden age of 'Hopping Down in Kent', when work in the hop gardens provided 'a happy and healthy working holiday' for London city dwellers. Quite forgotten were the signs of 'no dogs, gypsies or pickers' that had been too often displayed in Kent pubs. What does remain? Oast houses reused as dwellings plus the hops themselves, new varieties as well as great old varieties that are still used in beer production today. The most popular hops in Kent used in the twentieth century included Golding, a variety of the Canterbury hop which was developed by Mr Golding of East Malling, and Fuggles, said to have developed from a seed thrown from a hop-picking dinner basket on the farm of George Stace of Horsmonden in 1861 and commercially developed by Richard Fuggle of Brenchley about 1880. Earlier the Colgate variety, propagated from a plant found in a hedge in Chevening by Mr Colegate, was widely grown in the Weald. Wye College developed the Wye Target variety which was disease resistant.

So the farming and harvesting of the hop in Kent has been recorded in every kind of literary text – poems, practical farming manuals, songs, medical remedies and recipes for beer to name but a few. Starting in the twentieth century it was used more imaginatively in novels and plays in which the hop garden featured as an atmospheric backdrop to the fictional action. Today, the hop gardens are all but gone, the hoppers' huts have either been dismantled, are gently disintegrating or are being used to house migrant European farm workers, and the oast houses have become private dwellings. So within living memory much has been lost from the Kent and Sussex countryside. Yet the story of the hop has not yet ended.

This book is a personal selection from the massive amount of material available on the history, heritage and social context of hop farming in Kent and, to a lesser extent, Sussex.

Fran & Geoff Doel, 2014

Anne Hughes

'The Early Years of Hop Growing in Kent' (2002)

Anne and Bill Hughes moved to Paddock Wood in 1958 when hop picking was still part of the local scene, later relocating to Hadlow in 1969 when hops were still grown in the area. Anne fulfilled a long-held ambition by studying for a BA in History awarded in 2002, at the University of Kent Centre Tonbridge. The course included the Theory and Practice of Local History in a Diploma in Kentish History. The essay 'The Early Years of Hop Growing in Kent' was written at this time. Sadly, there is only one farm in the parish currently growing hops.

❧❧❧

Turkeys Carp, Hops, Pickerel and Beer,
came to England all in one Year.

This old rhyme, dating from 1424, has several variations, another being, 'Hops, Reformation, Bays and Beer', but all include hops. J.M. Russell in his *History of Maidstone* states that in 1424 information was laid against a person for 'putting into beer an unwholesome weed called a hoppe.' This would probably have been the wild hop, *humulus lupulus*, generally considered to have been brought to England by the Romans. The Roman naturalist Pliny told of hops growing in garden *culpes* as a weed and the Romans used the young shoots as a vegetable – a practice carried on by country people until recent times, one Hadlow lady likening it to asparagus. A 1440 dictionary *promptorium* includes 'Hoppe, sede for beeyre'. Culpeper's *Herbal* (1653) states that: 'The wild hop growth up as the other doth … but it giveth small heads in far less plenty.' He recommends its use in the form of a decoction of the tops, the tops and the flowers, powdered seed or a syrup of the juice against a wide variety of ailment including obstructions of the liver and spleen, to cure scabs, itch tetters, ringworm, spreading sores, the morphewe and all discolourings of the skin. Culpeper writes that 'both the wild and the manured are of one property, and alike affective…' but makes no mention of their use in beer. Perhaps he assumed his readers would be aware of this. Gerard's *Herbal* (1616) states 'the manifold virtues of Hops do manifestly argue the wholesomeness of beer above ale for the hops rather make it a physical drink to keep the body in health, than an ordinary drink for the quenching of our thirst.'

Until the mid-sixteenth century the common brew of Britain was ale, often seasoned with the spices clove and cinnamon, or plants such as wormwood and ground ivy. The Flemish weavers brought to England, particularly Kent by Edward III during the fourteenth century, were accustomed to lighter beer made with hops. It would seem likely that they would have imported their beer from the Continent, or perhaps the hops, eventually teaching local farmers to grow hops to enable them to brew beer to their own taste. This development must have gained in popularity, although not with the herbalists who saw their trade threatened. The records of Henry VIII's household at Eltham contain a 1530 instruction to the brewer not to put hops or brimstone in the ale as it was thought to 'dry up the body and increase melancholy'. The accounts of a wealthy household at Lestranges in Norfolk include several purchases of 'hoppys' in 1530. In spite of opposition, hop growing increased and Dr Joan Thirsk suggests that the government encouraged home-grown crops to replace imports.

No records remain to identify the site where the first hops were grown commercially, but tradition puts the first hop gardens in the parish of Westbere in 1520 or at Great Chart where grapes were replaced by hops during Henry VIII's reign. Dr Thirsk likens the early growers to 'pioneers'. Daniel Defoe in 1717 visited Maidstone and said: 'Here, likewise, and in the county adjacent, are great quantities of hops planted and this is called the Mother of Hop Grounds in England, being the first place in England where hops were planted in any quantity, and long before they were planted in Canterbury.'

William Harrison wrote in his 'Description of England' (1577):

Of late years we have found and taken up a great trade in planting of hops, whereof our more hitherto and unprofitable grounds do yield such plenty and increase that there are few farmers of occupiers in the country which have not gardens and hops growing of their own, and those far better than do come from Flanders unto us.

Kent's enclosed system of field farming, rather than the traditional system of open fields elsewhere, was easily adapted to the hops. Hedges surrounding the fields provided protection from the wind and the climate was generally favourable. There was plenty of wood for the poles and for fuel for drying the crop, and workers both local and from London to supply the seasonal labour needed. London also provided a market for surplus hops, with the River Medway useful as a means of transport. The farmers in Kent were also in a better position than others to fund the initial outlay for poles, etc. to plant up a hop garden.

In a good year, hops could be a profitable crop; John Worlidge of Hampshire suggested that in 1669 an acre or two of ground-growing hops would yield more profit than 50 acres of arable land, with less time, cost and expense needed.

During the reign of James I an Act was passed for 'avoyding of deceitfull selinge, buyinge or spenging corrupte and unwholesom Hoppes.' Hops found to be mixed with leaves, soil etc. to increase the weight would be forfeited. From 1710 only British hops could be imported into Ireland. In 1711 excise duty was a penny a pound, and customs duty threepence a pound. By 1734 excise duty of one penny a pound had been imposed. The grower also had to furnish details of his ground, oast and storage or give a penalty of forty shillings an acre. A £10 fine was to be imposed for re-bagging foreign hops into English pockets. A penalty of £40 was incurred for using more than one pocket bearing the mark of an excise officer.

There is little early evidence of individual hop gardens. Like grass and fruit, hops on the bine were not legally needed to be included in inventories, although the mention of hop poles and other items would indicate hop growing. A 1710 inventory in Leigh in Kent for John Wicking of Pauls Farm includes 3 acres of hop poles and two oasthairs. Although there is also a brewhouse and equipment, any hops grown could well have been for the family's personal use. William Walter of Tonbridge in 1713 had hop poles and other utensils worth £24, plus eleven bags of hops and three pockets weighing 27cwts worth £91 2s 6d. The inventory of James Taylor of Aylesford (1689) includes:

In the Oasthouse Chamber
Item one pocket of hopps, one oastheare and some other small things 01.03.00
Item eight bags of hopps 50.00.00
In the Barne
Item a stock of hoppoles for five acres and one yard of hopground 31.10.00

Farmers were not short of advice on hop growing. While Thomas Tusser made no mention of hops in his 1557 book *One Hundred Points of Good Husbandry*, by the time the sequel *Five Hundred Points of Good Husbandry* was published in 1573 he advised that 'hops hateth the land with gravel and sand'. The following year Reynolde (Reginald) Scot published *A Perfite Platforme of a Hoppe Garden* which was to be the standard work on hop cultivation for 200 years. Scot came from Smeeth near Ashford and had learned about hop growing through working with them. The book is well illustrated with woodcuts showing the various stages of cultivation, presumably for those less skilled in reading. He advised growing the plants on a small mound of earth, erecting three or four poles when the shoots appeared above the ground. The hops were to be tied to the poles with rushes or woollen material. The 3ft-high mounds of earth, flattened on the top, were to beat weeds. It was suggested that alders be planted to the north and east for shelter and to supply poles. Scot advised, 'Grow as much and no more than you can dispose of and do not be lured by the desire for profit to cultivate hops to excess.' He suggested that an acre of ground and the third part of a man's labour, plus small additional cost, would yield forty marks yearly to those that 'ordereth well' for the plants to climb up. Gervas Markham's *Inrichment of the Weald of Kent* (1631) also gave advice. Professor R. Bradley, Professor of Botany at Cambridge University, suggested in his book *Riches of a Hop-Garden Explained* (published 1725): 'Wherein such Rules are laid down for the Management of the Hop, as may improve the most barren ground, from one Shilling to thirty or forty Pounds an Acre per Annum.' He also gave practical advice on preparing the ground and harvesting.

Many visitors to England referred to the hops, including Celia Fiennes who in 1697 commented:

We pass by great Hopyards on both sides of the road (between Sittingbourne and Canterbury) and this year was great quantityes of that fruite here in Kent.

Thence to Rochester 8 mils, I came by a great many fine hopp-yards where they were at work puling the hopps.

The Swede Peter Kalm, in July 1748, showed a much more scientific interest. He wrote:

Hop-gardens

Most of them are at Canterbury, and then comes Maidstone. On 6 July I saw a man going into the Hopfield and tearing away all the lowest leaves from the hop – up to two ells from the ground – in order to stem the hop's growth. The cost of hop-gardens here in Kent is such that when all the expenses incurred by growing hops are added up for one year it comes to twenty-four or twenty-five pounds sterling or more, from seven or eight acres, after allowing for all expenses. But the management of hops is an uncertain trade. Often, when hops are at their greenest and most splendid one night can destroy them, so that the next day they are black. Often when the hops are completely ready to be taken down to be picked, one night can completely spoil the flowers, so that hardly any use can be made of them. This is thought to be caused by some sort of dew. As far as anyone knows, chalk has never been used to fertilise hops, but the fertiliser which they use most is burnt horse manure mixed with the dirt which collects on the roads, and this is reckoned to be the best. A hop-garden demands very rich earth. When it has once been fertilised it can stand three or four years before it needs doing again. The hop-gardens here were formed of tripods; one tripod was made from three sticks put into a triangle, with the tops of the triangles sticking out. There were about ten quarters between each tripod. In the string the tripods are taken down and the hopfields made flat; at this time the whole of the field is dug and hoed in order to get rid of the weeds, and after that the soil is heaped together for the three sticks, and the tripod is made. Between Gravesend and Rochester we saw a lot of hop-gardens, particularly around Rochester. Mostly they were planted on the south-east side of a chalk slope, and mostly on such slopes as were not very steep. They were in tripod, and usually two ells between each and the sticks came from all sorts of leaf trees. Because these fields were still unweeded the soil around the tripods was no higher than in the surrounding field. The tripods were arranged not *ordine quincunciali* but in squares … the hops were already much longer than the sticks and no flowers were yet in bloom. Some hop-gardens had been weeded so well that the soil between the tripods was like the tidiest garden plot.

The busiest time of the year was hop picking. According to the *Perpetual Almanack of Folklore*, hop picking began on 11 September, but Scot advises: 'What time your hops begin to change colour, somewhat before Michaelmas … you must gather them, and for the speedier despatch thereof procure as much help as you can, taking advantage of fair weather, and note that you were better to gather them too early than too late.'

Leonard Mascall's *Book of the Arte and manner, how to plant and Graffe all sortes of Trees* suggests picking 'at such time after Michaelmasse as ye shall see your hop waxe browne or somewhat yellow'. Opinion was divided as to picking close to the plants, or to take the bines indoors to pick, but all agreed that it was wiser to pick the hops when dry.

In the early years it is likely that picking was done by local helpers plus in some cases able-bodied poor from the workhouse, but as acreage grew, itinerant workers flooded into Kent. An epic poem of more than 700 lines by Christopher Smart, born in Shipbourne in 1722, includes this verse:

See, from the great metropolis they rush,
The industrias vulgar! They, like prudent bees
In Kent's wide garden road, expert to crop
The flowery hop, and provident to work
Ere winter numb their sunburnt hands.

The accounts of the 1743 harvest for Richard Tylden of Milstead list the names of hop pickers at each bin, including his wife and their servants. His total costs are shown as £7 6s 9d with hops sold for £18 2s 2d, plus a few shillings for hops apparently sold to locals, leaving 40lbs of hops for his own use.

There is a somewhat idealised engraving of hop picking in *English Hops*. In 1750 William Ellis in his *Modern Husbandman* gives a description of hop picking on a farm near the town of (West) Malling:

> Esquire Whitworth … has a hundred acres of Hop ground in which he runs up a little Hut or Shed, at every one or two Bins, and furnishes it with wheat straw for the Pickers to lie on, and a cask of small Beer, that they may not lose Time in Quest of Drink … This with a penny a bushel for Gathering and a Feast when the Hop-work is all done, makes their Hearts glad.

The influx of people would appear to have grown by 1786, if newspaper reports are anything to go by. The *Maidstone Journal* of 1786 reports: 'The number of tramps migrate to this county for the hop harvest, not meeting the advantages they expected from the badness of the hops, occasioned by the tempestuous weather etc., have been driven to commit burglaries in the neighbourhood.'

The *Publick Advertiser* a few weeks earlier had complained: 'They are sadly infested with a number of idle people, men and women, who come under the pretence of picking hops, or harvest work, and till they can get employment they support themselves by theft.'

The *Morning Chronicle* in August the same year reported that around Tonbridge, 'the hop pickers are now pouring in upon us from all quarters'.

W. Marshall in his *Rural Economy of the Southern Counties* observed in 1798 that:

> … the numerous throngs of workpeople with the attendant swarms of children which everywhere meet the eye, is particularly striking. Whole families, indeed the whole country, may be said to live in the fields during the busy season of hopping … it is the custom for women of almost every degree to assist at the hop-picking. The town of Maidstone is nearly deserted, in the height of the season. Tradesmen's daughters, even of the higher classes, and those of farmers and yeomen of the first rank and best education are seen busy at the hop bins.

John Byng passed through West Kent in 1790 and recorded that 'Every creature … was employed in picking hops, with their whole families.'

Pay was determined by the fullness of the crop and settled at so many bushels or baskets to the shilling. In some cases pickers were given hop tokens, marked with initials or numbers, in exchange for a certain volume of hops, to be redeemed later. Some examples of moulds for tokens are in Maidstone Museum. Another system was a tally with a piece of stick given to the picker, the tallyman marking a duplicate stick with the amount picked.

The hops were dried in a rectangular barn-like building, with the fresh hops stored at one end, the actual drying taking place in a kiln in the middle, the dried hops at the other end. Scot's book included a plan for such a building. Hops were sometimes dried in a malt kiln or even in an attic without artificial heat. A later development was for a square kiln to be built at one end. Specification for an oast house 40ft x 17ft for Augustine Taylor of Tonbridge has survived. Charcoal was used for heat to dry the hops and it was customary to hire the facilities out to smaller hop growers, as happened on the Camer estate near Meopham. The now familiar oast houses were not introduced until about 1835. Hop drying was a skilled job and an expert could expect double the normal wages during the season, and would have a generous supply of beer as it was hot and thirsty work.

There were weekly markets in Maidstone and Canterbury for the sale of Kent hops, but by 1681 a hop market was established in London, first in Little Eastcheap, then in Borough high street. An engraving of 1729 in *English Hops* shows hop pockets both in the market hall, the ground floor of the old town, and on carts.

The cloth industry would have benefited in a small way from the supply of fabric for hop pockets and oasthairs. Clinch suggests that a rough cloth was made from the fibre of the bines and used for bins and pokes, but this does not appear to be mentioned elsewhere. The woodland owners would also make considerable income from supplying hop poles, normally replaced after four years' use, in addition to wood for charcoal. Discarded hop poles were used for firewood. Blacksmiths would also have been employed in the manufacture of tools, some specifically designed for the task.

By 1700 about 3,000 acres were cultivated in Kent, representing at least one-third of the national output. Most were in plots of less than 2 acres, being part-time projects of townspeople and tradesmen. City dwellers often hired people to manage their hops. The return was about £10–15 per acre, or twice the outlay. A terrier of 1714 for Goudhurst shows thirty-one growers on 37 plots, 28 being under 2 acres and 9 less than 1 acre. Hop growing was as usual subordinate to mixed farming. A farm of 100 acres would use 8–10 acres for hops. Hops rated highly on the list of alternative crops between 1650 and 1750.

What of the final product, beer? Brewing had originally been carried out at home and on the farms usually by the women of the household. *The Compleat Housewife* by Eliza Smith originally published in 1758 contains a recipe for strong beer, which seems very time-consuming and complicated. Two bushels of malt and half a bushel of wheat are used for a barrel of beer, two pounds of hops and a handful of rosemary flowers. Later six eggs are added – presumably to clarify the liquid – and the mixture is left to stand for a year. Presumably this was a special type of beer, as no household would have had the space or equipment to brew all their needs in this way. English ale was traditionally very strong and sweet, which helped to keep it well. Hops acted as a preservative as well as flavouring, with lower strength and less sweetness. As demand increased, brewing took place in premises attached to individual taverns or alehouses. In 1577 a census of all taverns, inns and alehouses was taken for the purpose of a taxation scheme, and found there were 19,759, or one for every 187 people! During the Civil War, taxes were imposed on beer. Oliver Cromwell, the son of a brewer, eventually freed the domestic brewer from paying duty, but excise duty for commercial brewing remained. During the seventeenth century, many famous breweries began trading, such as Thrales Anchor Brewery, Southwark, in 1616 and Trumans in 1683. Other businesses still trading today are Whitbreads who began trading in 1742, Charringtons in 1766 and Courage in 1789. The invention of scientific instruments, including Fahrenheit's thermometer, and publications such as *The London and Country Brewer* and Michael Combrune's *Theory and Practice of Brewing* in the 1760s made the brewing process more reliable, while the introduction of isinglass for clarification shortened the time between brewing and readiness for drinking. The newly fashionable porter used more hops.

In the late seventeenth century brewing was a feature of the Kent economy. Navy victualling helped to sustain breweries in the Medway area. Commercial brewers were established in Margate, Rochester, Canterbury, Dover, Gravesend, Hythe and Maidstone before 1800 while a directory of 1832 records no less than five breweries in High Street, Chatham. By the nineteenth century virtually every town had at least one brewery. Hadlow's was owned by the Barton family. A document of 1710 refers to a 'malthouse newly erected' and in 1755 William Barton, described as a malster, inherited a malthouse and cider house. It would seem from the full description of the property that brewing was part of a larger farming business. Henry Barton, son of John Barton of Hadlow, is listed among the Brewers Company apprenticeships in 1733. The burial registers of St Mary's church, Hadlow, include Stephen, son of John Barton, cider maker in 1702 and William Barton, malster, dying in 1784 at the age of 70. Oliver Hodge Barton is shown as a brewer on the baptism of his daughters in 1824 and 1827.

Celebrating their 300th anniversary this year (1998) are Shepherd Neame of Faversham, who claim to be Britain's oldest brewers. While their official founding date is 1698, there is some evidence of earlier brewing on the site. The original founder, Richard Marsh, is included in a 1678 list of brewers paying dues in Faversham. The Shepherd family acquired the business in 1742, with Percy Neame becoming a partner in 1865. It claims to have used the same source of water throughout the centuries.

Throughout the seventeenth and eighteenth centuries the quantity of hops being grown in England increased and by 1800 there were some 35,000 acres under cultivation. Home Office reports in 1801 include hop growing in East Malling, Frittenden (a great many acres of hops), Leigh (371 acres of hops), Marden (600 acres of hops), Speldhurst (100 acres of hops) while Smarden has a 'considerable' hop acreage.

Hop cultivation was evident in my home village of Hadlow. Hasted's description of Hadlow states of the local soil: 'lower down it is much more fertile, and bears good corn, and is kindly for hops, of which there are many plantations, which have much increased of late years.' An account of the perambulation of the village boundaries in 1833 refers to a hop garden called Charity Barnfield, another on Horn's Lodge Farm, Mr Simmonds' hop garden, another once called Bates Meadow, Mr Kippings' hop garden, and Mr Golding's Bourne Field Hops. An earlier perambulation mentions Rounds' hop garden, a 4-acre hop garden, Mr Norwood's hop garden and Mr Martyr's Hop House.

Many of the farmers developed their own variety of hop, reflected in the names. Among these were James Tolhurst of Horsmonden, Iden Henham of East Peckham, George White of Hunton who introduced White's Early, Alfred Amos of Wye who favoured Amos's Early Bird, Bennett of Wrotham, Seale of Horsmonden, Bates of Brenchley, David Colegate of Chevening. Gerald Warde of Tutsham Hall developed Tutsham, while Prolific was reared by Thomas Guest of Chill Mill, Brenchley, from an earlier variety called Old Jones. Two varieties which survive to the present day are Fuggles, discovered by Richard Fuggle of Brenchley in a flower garden in Horsmonden and Golding, produced by Mr Golding of Malling in 1790.

For a full picture of hop growing round 1800, John Boys' *General View of the Agriculture of the County of Kent* goes into great detail of labour and equipment and their costs. Boys farmed on a large scale in the Sandwich area and would seem to have been very knowledgeable, both in the theory and practical side of farming, traditional and modern. He used 5 acres of land for growing wood for hop poles, calculating after eleven years that the value was £91 per acre on land worth 6–7s in rent. He advised that an area of 4–5 acres would require an oast 16ft square, costing £150–200. Picking baskets cost 5s 6d each, scales £5, a shim (similar to a wheelbarrow) £2 2s, a harrow £1 15s, an iron peeler to make holes and a 'dog' to wrench up poles 5s.

He suggested that the hills should be manured with twenty-five cartloads of manure – dung, mud and sand – per acre and left for a year. Rags could also be used at the rate of 1 ton per acre, costing £4–6 per ton. It seems that it was common to plant hops, cherries and filberts together, with 800 hop hills per acre. The hops were allowed to stand for twelve years, by which time the fruit trees were mature enough to grow on their own. Small poles were best for the first year, replaced by 15–20ft poles in the second year. He commented that the best poles had reached the enormous price of £3 per hundred, but had now fallen to 30s. Labour costs are also listed, including 15s to £1 for digging an acre, 5s per day for cutting, 2s for shaping poles, 10s a day for tying hops, 5s for summer hoeing.

Prices for hops varied considerably. In 1699 they fetched £4–7 a cwt, dropping to £1 15s in 1701, and gradually rising to £3 10s – £5 15s in 1790, and reaching £10 10s – £11 10s in 1793. Betting took place on hop duty and crop results, but attempts to rig the market were not allowed. In 1800 Samuel Ferrand Waddington who lived near Tonbridge was fined £500 with one month in prison for forestalling the hop market. He had bought a large number of hop gardens with a view to controlling the price.

From Cobbett's comments in his *Rural Rides* it can be seen that the expansion in hops continued: 'I passed by the side of a village called Horsenden and saw some very large hop-grounds away to my right. I should suppose there were fifty acres and they appeared to me to look pretty well.' At Hollingbourne he saw, 'By very far indeed, the finest piece of hops. A beautiful piece of hops, surrounded by beautiful plantations of your ash, producing poles for hop gardens.'

A few miles further on he comments of his journey from Maidstone to 'Merryworth' (Mereworth):

These are the finest seven miles that I have ever seen in England or anywhere else … From Maidstone to Merryworth I should think that there were hop-gardens on one half of the way on both sides of the road. Then looking across the Medway, you see hop-gardens and orchards two miles deep, on the side of a gently rising ground: and this continues with you all the way from Maidstone to Merryworth.

There are still some fine hops grown near Mereworth to this day. The hop-growers of the time, but not the woodsmen, could well have echoed Cobbett's dream: 'If I could discover *an everlasting hop-pole* and one, too, that would grow faster even than the ash, would not these Kentish hop-planters put me in the Kalendar along with their famous Saint Thomas of Canterbury?'

CHAPTER ONE

THE TUDOR HOPPE

Andrew Boorde (Borde)(1490–1549)

A Dyetry of Health (1542)

Andrew Boorde (also known as Borde) was a Tudor physician and his dislike of the newly introduced 'beer' which was flooding into England from the Low Countries seems to have been purely on health grounds. Before the advent of hop-flavoured beer, all men drank ale. It appears from Boorde's comments that the new beer's manufactory was in the hands of foreigners such as the Dutch. Traditional English ale (which Boorde considers much more wholesome than hopped beer) was 'a sweet, malty drink flavoured with herbs such as ale-hoof, wormwood and ground ivy'. This new drink, beer, he warned, will give you a big belly and may even kill you if you have certain medical conditions such as colic. Had he lived today, he would probably have recommended that a Government Health Warning accompany each pint sold.

Boorde's own life was quite extraordinary. At a young age he became a Carthusian, a hermit monk, whose lifestyle involved continual prayer, fasting and wearing a hair shirt. Finding this too rigorous, he managed, through the good offices of Thomas Cromwell, to get permission to leave his charterhouse and to engage in medical studies in Europe and later in Glasgow. Thomas Cromwell, Secretary of State for Henry VIII, appears to have subsequently employed Boorde as an 'intelligencer' (spy), possibly financing his numerous trips in Europe and even to Jerusalem, as a means of gauging opinion abroad on the king's recent divorce. While living in France, Boorde wrote a number of works, notable 'for their good sense and wit', including a continental guidebook and treatises on how to maintain a healthy lifestyle. After Cromwell was put to death for treason and heresy Boorde, having presumably lost his funding as well as his protector and benefactor, returned to England and made his home in Winchester but was later arrested and imprisoned in the Fleet, being accused of 'keeping in his house three loose women'. Whether these charges were fabricated or not, one of his detractors caustically mentioned that he had continued to fast as part of his chosen lifestyle in what was now Protestant England and to wear a hair shirt.

The following are Boorde's descriptions of ale and of the new drink, beer, along with his affirmation that 'I do drinke no manner of beere made with hopes'.

❧❧❧

of Ale

Ale is made of malte and water and they the which do put any other thynge to ale than is rehersed, except yest, barme, or godesgood, doth sofystical theyre ale. Ale for an Englysshe man is a natural drynke. Ale must have three propertyes: it must be fresshe and cleare. It must not be ropy nor smoky, nor must it have no weft nor tayle. Ale should not be dronke under v. dayes olde. New ale is vnwholesome for all men. And sowre ale, and dead ale the which doth stand a tylt, is good for no man. Barly malte maketh better ale than oten malte or any other come doth; it doth ingendre grose humoures; but yette it maketh a man strong.

of Bere

Bere is made of malte, of hoppes and water; it is a naturall drynke for a Dutche man. And now, of late dayes it is moche used in Englande, to the detriment of many Englysshe men; specially it killeth them the which be troubled with the colycke and the stone and the strangulio; for the drynke is a cold drynke; yet it doth make a man fat, and doth inflate the bely, as it doth appeare by the Dutche mens faces and belyes. If the bere be well served and be fyned and not new it doth qualify the heat of the lyver.

Thomas Tusser (1524–1580)

Five Hundred Pointes of Good Husbandrie (1557)

After the influx of religious refugees from Flanders in 1525 there is evidence of hop growing in England as Edward VI's Privy Council in 1549 made payments for charges in bringing over hop setters 'for planting and setting of hops'.

Thomas Tusser's work written in 1557 gives us written evidence of hops being cultivated specifically for brewing in Tudor England. Tusser advised farmers to earth the hops in mounds which had been treated with fertiliser and as the young hops grew, they were to be tied to small hop poles and the bines twisted onto strings. The running of the bine stalks took place in the early spring and from May to August was the growing season, the hops requiring plenty of sun and water. After harvesting the hops were to be quickly dried and packed.

The need for such a manual on hop husbandry in the mid part of the sixteenth century tells us that hop farming was being introduced and proving lucrative. It was certainly crucial in transforming many acres in Kent into hop-gardens.

Thomas Tusser was born in the reign of Henry VIII and died in the reign of Elizabeth I. As a boy he was a gifted chorister in St Paul's Cathedral. Later he was sent to Eton, and after this Cambridge – studying both at King's College and Trinity Hall. Tusser wrote this informative and highly enjoyable farming manual in verse while living as a gentleman farmer in Suffolk, and this is just some of his advice on the cultivation of the hop.

An early hop garden woodcut from Reynolde Scot's *A Perfite Platforme of a Hop Garden*, 1574. (Fran & Geoff Doel Collection)

A Lesson Where and When to Plant Good Hop Yard

Whom fancy perswadeth, among other crops,
To have for his spending sufficient of hops;
Must willingly follow, of choices to chuse,
Such lessons approved as skilful do use.

Ground gravelly, sandy, and mixed with clay,
Is naughty for hops, any manner of way;
Or if be mingled with rubbish and stone,
For dryness and barrenness, let it alone.

Chuse soil for the hop, of the rottenest mould,
Well dunged and wrought, as a garden plot should:
Not far from the water (but not overflown)
This lesson well noted, is meet to be known.

The sun in the south, or else southly and west,
Is joy to the hop, as a welcomed guest;
But wind to the north, or else northly east,
To hop is as ill, as a fray in a feast.

Meet plot for a hop-yard, once found as is told,
Make thereof account, as of jewell of gold:
Now dig it, and leave it the sun for to burn,
And afterwards fence it, to serve for that turn.

The hop for his profit, I thus do exalt,
It strengtheneth drink, and it favoureth malt;
And being well brewed, long kept it will last,
And drawing abide, if ye draw not too fast.

August's Abstract

If hops look brown
Go, gather them down;
But not in the dew,
For piddling with few.

Of hops this knack,
A many doth lack:
Once had thy will,
Go cover his hill.
Take hop to thy dole,
But break not his pole.

Learn here, thou stranger,
To frame hop manger.

Hop poles preserve
Again to serve.
Hop-poles, by and by,
Lay safe up to dry.
Lest poles wax scant,
New poles go plant.

The hop, kiln dri'd,
Will best abide.
Hops dri'd in loft,
Want tendance oft;
And shed their seed,
Much more than needs.

Hops dri'd, small cost,
Ill kept, half lost.
Hops quickly be spilt
Take heed if thou wilt.

Some come, some go,
This life is so.

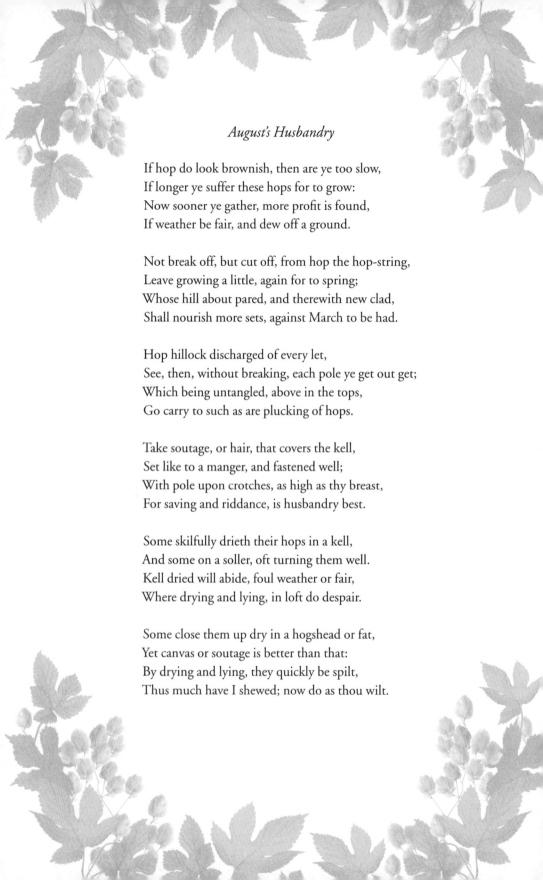

August's Husbandry

If hop do look brownish, then are ye too slow,
If longer ye suffer these hops for to grow:
Now sooner ye gather, more profit is found,
If weather be fair, and dew off a ground.

Not break off, but cut off, from hop the hop-string,
Leave growing a little, again for to spring;
Whose hill about pared, and therewith new clad,
Shall nourish more sets, against March to be had.

Hop hillock discharged of every let,
See, then, without breaking, each pole ye get out get;
Which being untangled, above in the tops,
Go carry to such as are plucking of hops.

Take soutage, or hair, that covers the kell,
Set like to a manger, and fastened well;
With pole upon crotches, as high as thy breast,
For saving and riddance, is husbandry best.

Some skilfully drieth their hops in a kell,
And some on a soller, oft turning them well.
Kell dried will abide, foul weather or fair,
Where drying and lying, in loft do despair.

Some close them up dry in a hogshead or fat,
Yet canvas or soutage is better than that:
By drying and lying, they quickly be spilt,
Thus much have I shewed; now do as thou wilt.

William Harrison (1534–1593)

Description of England (1577)

William Harrison was a distinguished scholar and Anglican clergyman who as an adult lived through the reigns of Mary and Elizabeth. He was household chaplain to Lord Cobham and rector of Radwinter in Essex, and later became canon at St George's Chapel, Windsor. In this last capacity he would have become well known to Queen Elizabeth and the court. When the queen's printer engaged various scholars to contribute to a vast tome (never completed in its entirety) which he prematurely and ambitiously entitled 'A Universal Cosmography of the Whole World', Harrison was invited to submit information on Britain and England. Harrison accordingly researched the great libraries of the day, drawing on books, letters, John Leland's notes, contemporary and antique maps, as well as from interviews with the most eminent antiquaries and local historians of the day such as John Stow and William Camden. To this he added his own observations and insights and produced a collection of scholarly notes which are not only admired today, but are recognised as giving us unparalleled insights into life in Elizabeth's day. These are some of his observations on 'Tudor' hops.

❧❧❧

From *Of Gardens and Orchards*

Hops in past time were plentiful in this land. Afterwards also their maintenance did cease. And now, being revived, where are any better to be found? Where any greater commodity to be raised by them? Only poles are accounted to be their greatest charge. But sith men have learned of late to sow ashen kexes in ashyards by themselves, that inconvenience in short time will be redressed.

From *Of the Food and Diet of the English*

The beer that is used at noblemen's tables in their fixed and standing house is commonly a year old, or peradventure of two year's tunning or more; but this is not general. It is also brewed in March, and therefore called March beer; but for the household, it is usually not under a month's age, each one coveting to have the same stale as he may, so that it might not be sour, and his bread as new as possible, so that it be not hot.

From *Of the Air and Soil and Commodities of the Island*

Of late years also we have found and taken up a great trade in planting of hops whereof our moory hitherto and unprofitable grounds do yield such plenty and increase that there are few farmers or occupiers in the country which have not gardens and hops growing of their own, and those far better than do come from Flanders unto us. Certes the corruptions used by Flemings, and forgery daily practised in this kind of ware, gave us occasion to plant them here at home; so that now we may spare and send many over unto them. And this I know by experience, that some one man by conversion of his moory grounds into hopyards, whereof before he had no commodity, doth raise yearly by so little as twelve acres in compass two hundred marks – all charges borne towards the maintenance of his family. Which industry God continue! Though some secret friends of Flemings let not to exclaim against this commodity, as a spoil of wood, by reason of the poles, which nevertheless after three years do also come to the fire, and spare their other fuel.

Reynolde Scot (1538–1599)

A Perfite Platforme of a Hoppe Garden (1574)

This English work devoted specifically to the cultivation of hops was by an author who had in 1582 produced a very different though equally influential book – though it was rejected by fanatics and famously angered James VI of Scotland (later James I of England) who ordered it to be burnt – an impressive review of fashionable contemporary beliefs about witches and witchcraft called The Discoverie of Witchcraft. *In this Scot suggested that the fascination with the persecution of witches should be rejected by all right-thinking men on the grounds of common sense and religion.*

Reginald (or Reynolde) Scot was a Kentish squire, the second son of Sir John Scot of Scots Hall in Smeeth. He lived during the reign of Elizabeth I and was himself a hop farmer. He had been schooled at Oxford but left without taking his degree. As a young adult he inherited and farmed lands in Smeeth as well as Brabourne in East Kent and later became MP for New Romney as well as a JP. In his farming manual A Perfite Platforme of a Hoppe Garden *which is illustrated with woodcuts, he deals with all the technical aspects of the business – the time to cut and set the roots and space out the hop-hills, the size and manner in which to erect the poles, what farm implements*

'The best and readyist Way to take the Hops from the Poles.' (From *A Perfite Platforme of a Hop Garden* by Reynolde Scot, 1574)

are needed, how to pick the hops, how to dry and pack the dried hops etc. It was a great success in its day mainly due to the simplicity of its style and helpful clarity of the illustrations, for he wished to 'write plainly to plain men of the country' in order that they should 'plant hops with effect'.

His work of course is not without its bias and shows, as Harrison's does, great antipathy towards the Flemings who, in introducing their 'bier' into England, were trying:

> to cram us with the wares and fruits of their country … dazzling us with the discommendation of our soil, obscuring and falsifying the order of this mystery, sending us to Flanders as far as Poppering for that which we may find at home in our own back sides.

Unlike Boorde, Scot is in favour of beer as a drink for the following reasons:

> In the favour of the Hoppe thus much more I say; that whereas you cannot make aboute above eight or nine gallons of indifferent Ale, out of one bushel of Malt, you may draw xviii or xx gallons of very good Beer, neither is the Hoppe more profitable to enlarge the quantity of your drinke, than necessary,

to prolong the continuance thereof. For if your Ale may endure fortnight, your Beere through the benefite of the Hoppe shall continuye a Month, and what grace it yieldeth is the Taste, all men may judge that have sense in their mouths, and if the controuerse be betwixt Beere and Ale, which of them two shall have place of preheminence: it sufficeth for the glorie and commendation of Beere that here in our own Country, Ale giveth place unto it, that most part of our Countrymen doe abhore and abandon Ales as a lothsome drincke, whereas in other nations Beere is of great estimation and of straungers entertained as ther most choice and delicate drinke. Finally that Ale which is more delicate and of best account, boroweth the Hoppe, as without the which it wanteth his chief grace and best verdure.

Scot advised farmers to carefully select the 'platforme' (site) for the garden, and to choose heavy soil which they knew to be rich. They should avoid exposed southerly-facing slopes, as storms from that direction were frequent in late summer, and the hop needed protection from 'violence and contagion of the wind' as well as plenty of sunshine. Scot saw a danger in over-production: 'Grow as much as and no more than you can dispose of and do not be lured by the desire for profit to cultivate hops to excess.'

Hop-pole puller, 1806. (Pyne, from the Fran & Geoff Doel Collection)

Nineteenth-century hop garden at Chartham. (Fran & Geoff Doel Collection)

The hop gardens in 1867 – 'Paying the Pickers'. (*Illustrated London News*)

Hop washing at Tonbridge, *c.*1890. (Fran & Geoff Doel Collection)

Above: Gypsy hop pickers, 1902. (Fran & Geoff Doel Collection)
Below: Hop pickers, *c*.1904. (Fran & Geoff Doel Collection)

Above: Hop pickers – one holding a horn – *c*.1904. (Fran & Geoff Doel Collection)
Left: Hop picking with baby. (Fran & Geoff Doel Collection)
Below: Hop pickers, *c*.1905. (Fran & Geoff Doel Collection)

Right: Hop pickers from Coolham, West Sussex. (Fran & Geoff Doel Collection)
Below: Picking into a basket while Talleyman looks on, *c*.1904 (the bines are climbing strings, and not the poles). (Fran & Geoff Doel Collection)

Below: Measuring the hops at Goudhurst. (Fran & Geoff Doel Collection)

Servicemen picking into bins. (Fran & Geoff Doel Collection)

Hop-picking family, 1920. (Fran & Geoff Doel Collection)

Right: Hop-pickers' bin at Cranbrook being emptied via the bushel-measuring basket into the poke for transport to the kiln. (Fran & Geoff Doel Collection)

Below: Hop pickers taking a tea break. The unnamed pipe-smoking lady photographed by A.W. Cullen was apparently a 'Celebrity on the Field of Action … a well-known figure for two score years in the hop fields, who claimed to own a brewery'. (Fran & Geoff Doel Collection)

Bottom: Hop picker being shaved (early Encyclopedia). (Fran & Geoff Doel Collection)

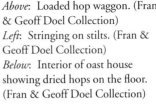

Above: Loaded hop waggon. (Fran & Geoff Doel Collection)
Left: Stringing on stilts. (Fran & Geoff Doel Collection)
Below: Interior of oast house showing dried hops on the floor. (Fran & Geoff Doel Collection)

Left: 'Hop Pickers': Talleymen. Tinted postcard, *c*.1910. (Fran & Geoff Doel Collection)

Below: Kentish hop picking: measuring the hops. Tinted postcard, *c*.1910. (Fran & Geoff Doel Collection)

Hop-pickers' encampment near Maidstone, showing gypsy caravans. Tinted postcard, *c.* 1910. (Fran & Geoff Doel Collection)

Hartlake Bridge from the *Illustrated London News*, 1853. (Fran & Geoff Doel Collection)

Right: Early postcard of hop-picking in Kent. (Fran & Geoff Doel Collection)
Below: Early painting of hop-pole pullers from a postcard. (Fran & Geoff Doel Collection)

Right: Kent hop pickers, *c*.1890.
(W.H. Boyer)
Below: Hops on their way
to market. (Fran & Geoff Doel
Collection)

Above: Little Hoppers' Hospital. (Fran & Geoff Doel Collection)

Right: Hoppers' huts at the Museum of Kent Life. (Fran & Geoff Doel Collection)

Below: Hoppers' huts (1860) from North Frith Farm, Hadlow, at the Museum of Kent Life. (Fran & Geoff Doel Collection)

Above: Hops near Finchcocks.
(Fran & Geoff Doel Collection)
Right: Hops at the Museum of
Kent Life. (Fran & Geoff Doel
Collection)
Below: Castle Farm Oast,
Sissinghurst. (Oast House Archive)

Above: Oast house, Batemans. (Fran & Geoff Doel Collection)
Left: The Oasts Gate, Court Farm, Northiam. (Oliver Nash)
Below left: Oast Theatre, Tonbridge. (Fran & Geoff Doel Collection)
Below: Oast houses, Powder Mill Lane, Hildenborough. (Fran & Geoff Doel Collection)

CHAPTER TWO

THE SEVENTEENTH-CENTURY HOP

Gervase Markham(1568–1637)

The English Husbandman (1613)

Gervase Markham was the third son of Sir Robert Markham of Cotham in Northamptonshire but he was born just as the family fortunes were failing disastrously. As a young man Markham decided to pursue a military career, serving as a soldier in the Low Countries. This was followed by service in Ireland under the Earl of Essex in which he greatly distinguished himself and was made commander. After the Essex rebellion Markham was called to the Elizabethan court but here his relationship with Essex was a bar to his advancement, despite his entertaining and brilliant feats of horsemanship in the much enjoyed tournaments and tilts before the queen and court where he passed 'a lance with much success'. As debts became pressing he decided, albeit reluctantly, to leave the court and to write for a living. When he retired from court he wrote extensively on practical husbandry, forestry and horsemanship (he was a famed horse-breeder and ran smallholdings). Because he excelled at Latin and had a good command of European languages he also produced a number of good Latin translations, translations from French and books of poems. Despite his prolific output and success with the reading public he did not make the hoped-for fortune. His most famous book is arguably The English Housewife *in which he instructs the seventeenth-century housewife how to cook, bake, brew, grow hemp and flax for spinning and, because the housewife had to care 'for the health and soundness of the body' of her family, supplies her with remedies to cure all ills including bad breath, the prevention of baldness, consumption and the plague.*

The following is from The English Husbandman.

❧❧❧

On the gathering of Hoppes …

Touching the gathering of Hoppes, you shall vnderstand that after Saint Margaret's day they begin to blossome, if it be in hot and riche soyles, but otherwise not till Lammas, in the worst at Michaelmas, and in the best earth they are full ripe at Michaelmas, in the worst at Martillmas; but to know when they are ripe indeede, you shall perceiue the seede to loose his greene colour, and looke as browne as a Hares backe, wherefore then you shall with all diligence gather them, and because they are a fruit that will endure little or no delay, as being ready to fall as soone as they be ripe, and because the exchange of weather may breede change in your worke, you shall vpon the first aduantage of faire weather, euen as soe as you shall see the dewe exhaled and drawe from the earth, get all the ayde of Men, Women and children which haue any vnderstanding, to helpe you, and then hauing some conueient empty barne, or shedde, made either of boards or canuas, neare to the garden, in which you shall pull your Hoppes, you shall then beginne at the nearest part of the garden and with a sharpe garden knife cut the stalkes of the Hoppes asunder close by the toppes of the hils; and then with a straite fork or iron, made broad and sharpe, for the purpose shere vp all the Hoppes and leave the poales naked. Then hauing labouring persons for the purpose let them carry them vnto the place where they are to be puld ad in any case cut no more than presently is caryed away as fast as they are cut, least if a shower of raine should happen to fall, and those being cut and taking wet, are in danger of spoyling. You shall prouide that those who pull your Hoppes be person of good discretion, who must not pull them one by one, but stripe them roundly through their hands into baskets, mixing the young buds and small leaues with them, which are as good as any paart of the Hoppe whatsoeuer. After you haue pulled all your Hoppes and carried them into svch conuenient dry rooms as you haue prepared for that purpose, you shall then spreade them vpon cleane floares so thinne as may be that the ayre may pass thorrow them, least lying in heaps they sweat and so mould, before you can haue leasure to dry them. After your Hoppes are thus ordered you shall then cleanse your garden of all such Hoppe straw ad other trash, as in the gathering was scattered therein: then hall you plucke vp all your Hoppe-poales in manner before shewed, and hauing either some dry boarded house, or shed, made for the purpose, pile them vpon another, safe from wind or weather.

In The English Housewife, *Markham's cure for the 'flux' is to 'take a stag pizzle' (penis), grate it and offer it to the patient in beer. Markham's other remedies which include beer promise a cure for the following conditions: ague, 'film over the eye', quinsy, stitch, yellow jaundice, 'hot and burning urine,' pissing in bed, consumption and 'all kinds of pestilential fevers'. He also suggests that a sauce made with beer, salt and breadcrumbs makes a tasty sauce 'for an old hen'.*

Nicholas Culpeper (1616–1654)

The Complete Herbal (1653)

Nicholas Culpeper was a doctor and a Puritan who lived in the first half of the seventeenth century. The son of a clergyman he was educated at Cambridge which he followed by a seven-year apprenticeship to an apothecary. A rich marriage permitted him to set up for himself and he chose to locate his practice 'outside the city walls' so that he could not be controlled by the City Fathers. He did not accept a fee for his medical consultations (he counselled over forty patients every morning) and collected his herbs in person from the surrounding countryside. The conceit and greed of his fellow physicians in London annoyed him and he referred to them as 'insulting' and 'insolent' men. After years of collecting and studying plants 'in the field' he enraged the medical fraternity when he published his work The English Physician *in English, for it brought a knowledge of medicine to the poorer section of the people and hence deprived the medical profession of fees. The* Herbal *was deliberately sold very cheaply and proved enormously popular but in the early days of the Civil War a charge of witchcraft was brought against him by the Society of Apothecaries which greatly damaged his reputation. Culpeper was fatally wounded while working as a field surgeon at the first Battle of Naseby and died in 1654 at the early age of 37.*

The Complete Herbal *follows the usual pattern of* Herbals *in that it gives an illustration and textual description of each plant, where it is to be found and its medicinal virtues.*

❧❧

From *The Complete Herbal*:

HOPS

Hops: These are so well known that they need no description; I mean the manured kind, which every good husband or housewife is acquainted with.

Description: The wild hop grows up as the other doth, ramping upon trees or hedges, that stand next to them, with rough branches and leaves like the former, but it gives smaller heads, and in far less plenty than it, so that there is scarcely a head or two seen in a year on divers of this wild kind, wherein consists the chief differences.

Place: They delight to grow in moist low grounds, and are found in all parts of this land.

Time: They spring not until April, and flower not until the latter end of June; the heads are not gathered until the middle or latter end of September.

Government and virtues: It is under the dominion of Mars. This, in physical operations, is to open obstructions of the liver and spleen, to cleanse the blood, to loosen the belly, to cleanse therein from gravel and provoke urine. The decoction of the tops of Hops, as well of the tame as the wild, works the same effects. Inn cleansing the blood they help to cure the French diseases and all manner of scabs, itch and other breakings-out of the body; as also all tetters, ringworms, and spreading sores, the morphew and all discolouring of the skin. The decoction of the flowers and hops, do help to expel poison that ay one hath drank. Half a dram of the seed in powder taken in drink, kills worms in the body, brigs down women's courses, and expels urine. A syrup made of the juice and sugar, cures the yellow jaundice, eases the head-ache that comes of heat, and tempers the heat of the liver and stomach, and is profitably given in long and hot agues that rise in choler and blood. Both the wild and the manured are of one property, and alike effectual in all the aforesaid diseases. By all these testimonies, beer appears to be better than ale. Mars owns the plant and then Dr Reason will tell you how to perform these actions.

These are some of Culpeper's remedies for medicines using hops:

Lupulus. Hops: Opening, cleansing, provoking urine; the young sprouts open stoppings of the liver and spleen, cleanse the blood, clear the skin, helps scabs, and itch, help agues, purge choler: they are usually boiled and taken as they eat asparagus, but if you would keep them, for they are excellent for those diseases, you may make them into a conserve, or into a syrup.

A purge for Spring: If in the Spring-time you use the herbs before-mentioned (Agrimony, Wormwood, Dodder, Hops and some Fennel, with Smallage, Endive and Succory-roots) and will take but a handful of each of them, and to them add an handful of Elder buds, and having bruised all, boil them in a gallon of ordinary beer, when it is new; and having boiled them half an hour, add to them three gallons more and let them work together, and drink a draught every morning, half pint or thereabouts; it is an excellent purge for the Spring, to consume the phlegmatic quality the Winter hath left behind it, and withal to keep your body in health, and consume those evil humours which the beat of Summer will really stir up. Esteem it as a jewel.

Chapter V: Directions for making Sirups &tc:
The young hop sprouts, which appear in March and April being mild, if boiled and served up like asparagus, are a very wholesome as well as pleasant tasted spring food. They purify the blood, and keep the body gently open.

Celia Fiennes (1662–1741)

Through England on a Side Saddle in the Time of William and Mary (c.1690)

Celia Fiennes was the daughter of a Parliamentarian supporter, Nathaniel Fiennes, a colonel in Cromwell's army during the English Civil War, and, like Cromwell, a gentleman, being the second son of a viscount, and educated at Winchester and New College, Oxford. After the Long Parliament was suspended her father took no more part in political life or the Restoration and lived quietly in the south of England. Celia was one of four daughters he had by his second wife, Frances. She was born only two years after the restoration of Charles and three years before plague and fire hit London. At the age of 22 and unmarried, Celia undertook an extraordinary series of journeys, almost all on horseback, which in those days was side-saddle for a woman, and accompanied only by one or two servants. Although she claimed that these lengthy visits were for her 'health by variety and change of aire and exercise' they would by their very nature have been quite arduous, for travel was notoriously difficult in the seventeenth century when roads were often unmade or simple dirt tracks. Highwaymen were an additional hazard on lonely stretches – yet she travelled through every county in England and in 1698 went even further afield and visited Scotland.

These are some of her observances regarding the cultivation of the hops in Kent. The diary was eventually published in the nineteenth century when a female relative, Emily W. Griffith, supplied this preface:

The account of several journeys through England undertaken by my kinswoman, Celia Fiennes, in the reign of William and may prove interesting as showing the manners and customs of those times. The writer's diligent and attentive observation of details concerning the various counties through which she passed either on horseback or in her equipage, and her descriptions … seem worthy of note and preservation … there being little literature of this kind and period in existence, Celia Fiennes's diary almost takes the position and value of an historical document, the only actual date mentioned is 1695. The absence of roads strikes one, and also the description of what is now the great manufacturing districts of the north. The original manuscript given to me by my father, has been copied verbatim, as I believe any correction or alteration would spoil its quaint originality. Celia Fiennes was the daughter of Nathaniel Fiennes, a Parliamentarian Officer, by the marriage with Miss Whitehead, and was sister of the third Viscount Saye and Sele.

From the diary:

Thence to Canterbury, 16 mile, we pass by great Hop yards on both sides of the Road, and this year was great quantetyes of that fruite here in Kent. There is a great number of French people in this town (Canterbury) wch are Employ'd in the weaving and silk winding. I meet them Every night going home in great Companyes, but then some of them are Employed in the Hopping, it being the season for pulling them.

From Canterbury its 30 mile to Maidstone. Maidstone town is a very neate market town as you shall see in the County, its buildings are mostly of timber worke, the streets are Large ... There is also a Large Gail. This streete notwithstanding the hall and Cross stands in the midst, is yet a good breadth and runs down a great Length quite to the bridge Cross the Medway which is not very broad here, yet it beares Barges that bring up burdens to the town ... This was Market day being Thursday and it seemed to be well furnish'd wth all sorts of Commodityes ... they told me it was not so full a Market as some dayes because the Country people were taken up aboute their hopping so Could not bring things to Market. Thence to Rochester 8 mile. I came by a great many ffine hopp yards where they were at work pulling ye hops. I came into Rochester at the other side, thro' the wood on the hill.

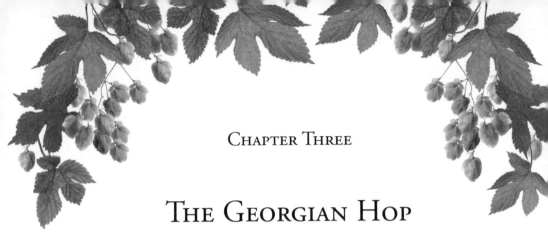

Chapter Three

The Georgian Hop

Daniel Defoe (1660–1731)

A Tour through the whole island of Great Britain, divided into circuits or journies (1724–27)

Daniel Foe (he adopted the name Defoe) is today celebrated as being one of the great pioneering eighteenth-century novelists along with Sterne, Richardson, Smollett, Swift and Fielding but in his day he gained notoriety as a political pamphleteer. Because of his political writings, in 1703 he was arrested and brought for trial at the Old Bailey, accused of seditious libel by powerful High Church Tories. Having been found guilty he was pilloried and imprisoned which occasioned one of his biographers to claim that 'no man in England but Defoe ever stood in the pillory and rose to eminence among his fellow men'.

The Tour of Great Britain *which he made on horseback was first published in three volumes between the years 1724 and 1727 and the true reason for undertaking the journey which was made before 1702 may have been to spy for William III.*

From Letter II, part I. Kent coast and Maidstone:

This (Maidstone) is a considerable town, very prosperous and the inhabitants generally wealthy: 'tis the county town, and the River Medway is navigable to it by large hoys, of fifty or sixty tuns burthen, the tide flowing quite up to the town; round this town are the largest cherry orchards, and the most of them that are in any part of England; and the gross of quantity of cherries, and the best of them which supply the whole city of London come from hence and are therefore called Kentish cherries.

Here likewise, and in the country adjacent, are great quantities of hops planted, and this is called the Mother of Hop Grounds in England; being the first place in England where hops were planted in any quantity; and long before any were planted at Canterbury ; though that be now supposed to be the chief place in England, as shall be observed in its place. These were the hops, I suppose, which were planted at the beginning of the Reformation and which gave occasion to that old distich:

Hops, Reformation, bays and beer
Came to England all in a year.

From Letter II, part II. Canterbury and Sussex:

The great wealth and increase of the City of Canterbury is from the surprising increase of the hop grounds all round the place; it is within memory of many inhabitants now living, and that none of the oldest neither, that there was not an acre of ground planted with hops in the whole neighbourhood, or so few as not to be worth naming; whereas I was assured that there are at this time near 6,000 acres of ground so planted, within a few miles of the city; I do not vouch the number and I confess it seems incredible, but I deliver as I receive it.

It is observed that the ground round the city proves more particularly fruitful for the growth of hops than of any other production, which was not at first known, but which upon its being discovered, set all the world speaking in the language of the neighbourhood, a digging up the grounds and planting; so that now they may say without boasting, there is at Canterbury the greatest plantation of hops in the whole island.

Song

'The Jovial Man of Kent (When Autumn Skies are Blue)'

This hopping song is found in Chappell's Old English Ditties *and the lyrics are thought to be by Charles Dibdin senior. The tune comes from the well-known old southern English song 'The Seven Trades' or 'The Jovial Crew'. 'The Jovial Man of Kent' was recorded by the Kent duo 'Tundra' on their* A Kentish Garland *record (SFA 078) and is currently (2014) in the repertoire of Kent singers Alan Austen, Roger Resch and one of the authors of this book, Geoff Doel.*

Well it's away with all wine drinkers
And all such fickle thinkers
And may they all be shrinkers
From all good men and true.
Thus spoke the jovial Man of Kent
As through the golden hops he went,
With sturdy limb and brow unbent,
When Autumn skies were blue above,
When Autumn skies were blue.

The hop that swings so lightly
And the hop that glows so brightly
Will surely be honoured rightly
By all good men and true.
Let the Frenchmen boast their straggling vine
Which gives them draughts of meagre wine,
It'll never match this bine of mine,
When Autumn skies were blue above,
When Autumn skies were blue.

Now when the Winter snows are falling
And the Winter winds are brawling
For the nut-brown they'll be calling
Those honest men and true.
And when their merry song is sung
And Yule logs on the fire are flung
They'll think upon the hops that swung,
When Autumn skies were blue above,
When Autumn skies were blue.

Hop garden watercolour by Essenhigh Corke, *c.* 1906. (Fran & Geoff Doel Collection)

Christopher Smart (1722–1771)

The Hop Garden (1752)

Though not published until 1752, 'The Hop Garden' was originally written for A Collection of Original Poems *in 1748 and brought this intense and highly original young poet into the public eye. At that point Smart was studying at Pembroke College, Cambridge, later to become a Fellow. The other entries in this prolific young scholar's collection were very different –* The Judgement of Midas, *a Masque, odes, some translations into Latin and some original poems in Latin. Although he continued to have links with Cambridge, Smart married and set up home in London where he embarked on a career as a writer. Between the years 1753 and 1755 Smart published seventy-nine works (many of them satirical or comic) and became the editor of a weekly paper, but despite his prolific output the money generated was not enough to maintain his young family and Smart subsequently became mentally ill, possibly through stress. Two years later, Smart was committed to a private hospital for the insane in Bethnal Green. His illness took the form of prolonged extempore prayer (usually in the street and on his knees), occasioning Dr Johnson's comment: 'I'd as lief pray with Kit Smart as anyone else.' Although released from the asylum in 1763 he was later confined in a debtors' prison where he died.*

Hop-pickers. (Fran & Geoff Doel Collection)

'The Hop Garden' is a glorification of 'the garden of England', full of classical allusions, in which the hop poles are stacked 'in comely cones' and the fruit picked by 'the hurrying peasant', and dried in the kiln attended by 'the sable priests of Vulcan'. On a less classical note is Smart's reference to one of the oldest recorded rituals in the Kentish Hop Garden – people (usually young men and women) being tossed up in a hop pocket particularly at the end of the harvesting. A hop-pocket consisted of a sturdy bin cloth attached to two solid wooden runners and was 6ft long and 2ft wide. Few suffered any hurt as the 'pocket' was normally left half-full of hops so that the fall was cushioned. George Orwell went hop picking in the early '30s as a prelude to using his experiences for a novel and called it a 'queer' game and an 'old' custom.

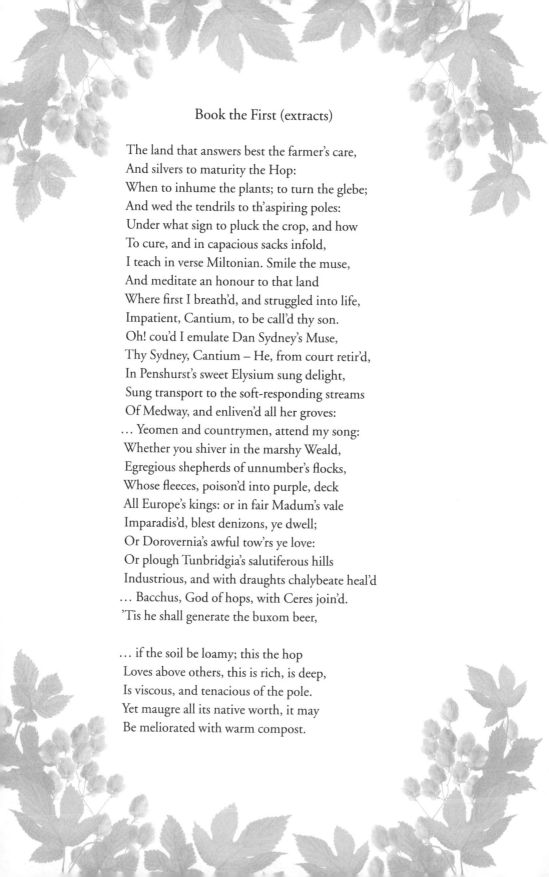

Book the First (extracts)

The land that answers best the farmer's care,
And silvers to maturity the Hop:
When to inhume the plants; to turn the glebe;
And wed the tendrils to th'aspiring poles:
Under what sign to pluck the crop, and how
To cure, and in capacious sacks infold,
I teach in verse Miltonian. Smile the muse,
And meditate an honour to that land
Where first I breath'd, and struggled into life,
Impatient, Cantium, to be call'd thy son.
Oh! cou'd I emulate Dan Sydney's Muse,
Thy Sydney, Cantium – He, from court retir'd,
In Penshurst's sweet Elysium sung delight,
Sung transport to the soft-responding streams
Of Medway, and enliven'd all her groves:
… Yeomen and countrymen, attend my song:
Whether you shiver in the marshy Weald,
Egregious shepherds of unnumber's flocks,
Whose fleeces, poison'd into purple, deck
All Europe's kings: or in fair Madum's vale
Imparadis'd, blest denizons, ye dwell;
Or Dorovernia's awful tow'rs ye love:
Or plough Tunbridgia's salutiferous hills
Industrious, and with draughts chalybeate heal'd
… Bacchus, God of hops, with Ceres join'd.
'Tis he shall generate the buxom beer,

… if the soil be loamy; this the hop
Loves above others, this is rich, is deep,
Is viscous, and tenacious of the pole.
Yet maugre all its native worth, it may
Be meliorated with warm compost.

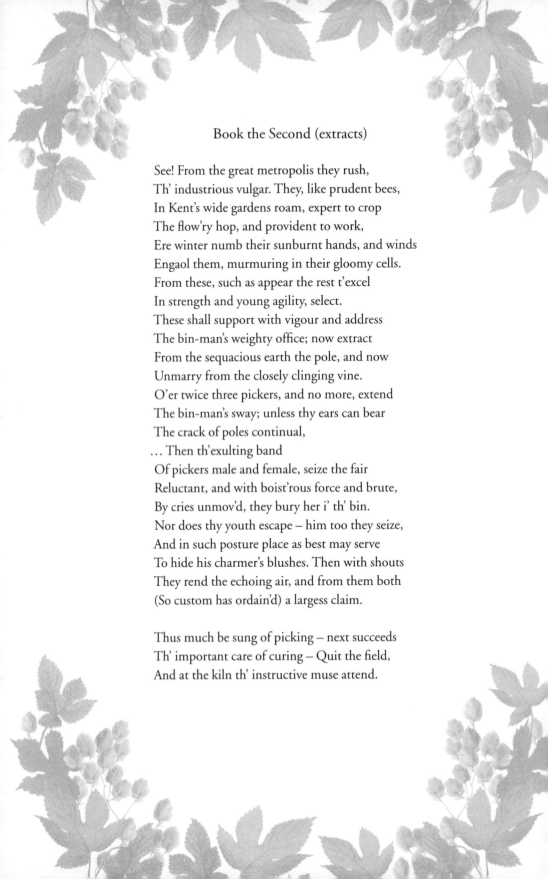

Book the Second (extracts)

See! From the great metropolis they rush,
Th' industrious vulgar. They, like prudent bees,
In Kent's wide gardens roam, expert to crop
The flow'ry hop, and provident to work,
Ere winter numb their sunburnt hands, and winds
Engaol them, murmuring in their gloomy cells.
From these, such as appear the rest t'excel
In strength and young agility, select.
These shall support with vigour and address
The bin-man's weighty office; now extract
From the sequacious earth the pole, and now
Unmarry from the closely clinging vine.
O'er twice three pickers, and no more, extend
The bin-man's sway; unless thy ears can bear
The crack of poles continual,
... Then th'exulting band
Of pickers male and female, seize the fair
Reluctant, and with boist'rous force and brute,
By cries unmov'd, they bury her i' th' bin.
Nor does thy youth escape – him too they seize,
And in such posture place as best may serve
To hide his charmer's blushes. Then with shouts
They rend the echoing air, and from them both
(So custom has ordain'd) a largess claim.

Thus much be sung of picking – next succeeds
Th' important care of curing – Quit the field,
And at the kiln th' instructive muse attend.

On your hair-cloth eight inches deep, nor more,
Let the green hops lie lightly; next expand
The smoothest surface with the toothy rake.
Thus far is just above; but more it boots
That charcoal flames burn equally below,
The charcoal flame, which from thy corded wood,
Or antiquated poles, with wond'rous skill,
The sable priests of Vulcan shall prepare.
Constant and moderate let the heat ascend;
Which to effect, there are, who with success
Place in the kiln the ventilating fan.

… When the fourth hour expires, with careful hand
The half-bak'd hops turn over. Soon as time
Has well exhausted twice two glasses more,
They'll leap and crackle with their bursting seeds,
For use domestic, or for sale mature.

… What then remains unsung? Unless the care
To stack thy poles oblique in comely cones,
Lest rot or rain destroy them – 'Tis a sight
Most seemly to behold, and gives, O Winter!
A landskip not unpleasing ev'n to thee.

… And as the oak reigns lordly o'er the shrub,
So shall the hop have homage from the vine.

Thomas Turner (1729–1793)

Diary for the Years 1754–65

Thomas Turner was born in the parish of Groombridge in 1729 where his father was a shopkeeper. Later he moved to the village of East Hoathly, in Sussex (his house still exists) and here, from the age of 24 and for the next eleven years, Thomas kept a journal.

Thomas ran and later was affluent enough to buy a general store in East Hoathly. In his shop, a 'mercers', he sold all manner of groceries and ironmongery as well as items of clothing. His parents by then were living in a neighbouring village, Framfield, and were also mercers.

Thomas's value to the community seems enormous. In addition to his work as a shopkeeper, Thomas worked as a part-time schoolmaster and local undertaker. He also assisted the more affluent in the community to manage their accounts and helped neighbours write wills. He additionally did all kinds of jobs for the parish including the tracking down of fathers of local unmarried girls who found themselves pregnant. In the summer he played cricket for his local team.

His diary indicates that hop picking was very much a local activity and that the community was involved at all levels.

Twice he mentions that hop pole pullers had called into his shop in 1765 to buy neckcloths. This was in September which is when the hop picking season starts and he mentions the two local farms involved – Mr Porter's and Hallands Hall. Hallands was at that time the seat of the Duke of Newcastle and an old Jacobean country house:

20 September

In the even, Mr Porter's hopers bought their pole-puller's nickcloth.

23 September

Halland hop pickers bought their pole-puller's nickcloth; and poor wretches, many of them insensible.

Scarlet neckerchiefs 'knotted round the throat' are frequently mentioned as being worn by male pullers throughout the nineteenth century and are often seen in illustrations and later photographs. No doubt pole pulling – which involved the 'cutting of the hop bines and lifting the supporting poles out of the ground in order to bring them low enough to be stripped by the pickers' – was hard sweaty work, but the bright colour could also pinpoint where a man was working in the hop field. One writer claimed that it gave a 'bright and oddly foreign effect among the bines'. The reference to the 'insensible' hop pickers may indicate that the hoppers were seriously drunk. Heavy drinking was a grievous problem in the eighteenth century. Turner himself was frequently inebriated as he records in his diary, but he often deeply regretted the drunken bouts and shenanigans after a night of carousing, as can be determined by this entry for 1758:

25 February

This morning about six o'clock just as my wife was got to bed, we was awakened by Mrs. Porter, who pretended she wanted some cream of tartar; but as soon as my wife got out of bed, she vowed she should come down. She found Mr. Porter, Mr Fuller and his wife, with a lighted candle, and part of a bottle of wine and a glass. The next thing was to have me downstairs, which being apprized of, I fastened my door. Up stairs they came, and threatened to break it open; so I ordered the boys to open it, when they poured into my room; and as modesty forbid me to get out of bed, so I refrained; but their immodesty permitted them to draw me out of bed, as the common phrase is, topsy-turvey; but, however, at the intercession of Mr Porter, they permitted me to put on my [drawers?] and instead of my upper cloaths they gave me time to put on my wife's petticoats; and in this manner they made me dance, without shoes and stockings, until they had emptied the bottle of wine, and also a bottle of my beer.

… About three o'clock in the afternoon they found their way to their respective homes, beginning to be a little serious, and, in my opinion, ashamed of their stupid enterprise and drunken perambulation.

On one occasion Turner found himself personally responsible for paying a number of hop pickers (all female) for 'three quarters of a day's picking'. All but two received 6d, whilst Dame Vinel only earned 4d and Molly Tomkin, presumably a child, was given 2d.

His diary mentions that after the harvest on a number of occasions he set out to buy bagged hops from local hop factors and is apparently in partnership with others in this venture – but whether he is selling them on or using them to brew his own beer to sell or for personal consumption is not clear.

There is one reference to Turner attending a hopping supper at the end of the hop harvest:

Wednesday, 18 September 1756

Went up to Master Piper, his hopping supper being tonight, where we supped on a forequarter of lamb roasted, a loin of lamb roasted, a mutton pie, plum pudding, carrots and cucumber (in company I dare say of 20 persons).

It may be that his interest in hops and love of beer did not abate as in later life Turner bought and ran the main public house in East Hoathly.

Eighteenth-century Cookbook

To Choose Hops

Rub them between the fingers or the palm of the hand, and if good, a rich glutinous substance will be felt, with a fragrant smell, and a fine yellow dust will appear. The best colour is a fine olive green, but if too green, and the seeds are small and shrivelled, they have been picked too soon and will be deficient in flavour. If of a dusty brown colour they were picked too late, and should not be chosen. When a year old, they are considered as losing one-fourth in strength. The best and dearest is the Farnham hop; East Kents are the next, but those of Sussex and Worcestershire are not so strong.

Eighteenth-century Cookbook

To Restore Musty Beer

Run it through some hops that have been boiled in strong wort and afterwards work it with double the quantity of new malt liquor: or if the fault is in the cask, draw it off into a sweet cask, and having boiled half a pound of brown sugar in a quart of water, add a spoonful or two of yeast before it is quite cold, and when the mixture ferments, pour it into the cask.

Song

'Hops': A New Song for the Year 1776

From the Kentish Gazette, *4 September 1776 and addressed to the farmers of Kent. Set to the tune of 'As I was a driving my Waggon one day', hopping songs were often set to existing tunes. This newly composed song exhibits no knowledge whatsoever of hopping:*

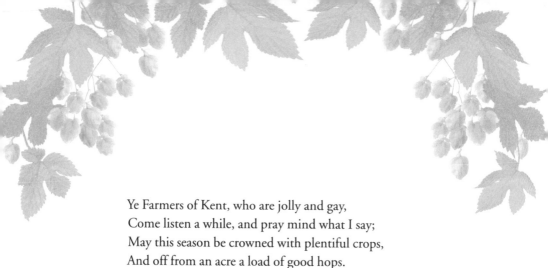

Ye Farmers of Kent, who are jolly and gay,
Come listen a while, and pray mind what I say;
May this season be crowned with plentiful crops,
And off from an acre a load of good hops.
    Geho, Dobbin, &c.

Oh! May they prove fine too, and fetch a great price,
That ye, my brave boys, may get rich in a trice;
For, as ye are ever both hearty and free,
Success to ye all, for to fill ye with glee!
    Geho Dobbin, &c.

To crown your repast in the hopping this year,
I wish that the weather may be fine and clear;
For when it is wet, it is wretched and sad,
From morning till night in a hop-ground to pad.
    Oh! Sad hopping &c.

Then to see the poor hoppers, alas! What a sight,
'Tis enough to put modesty into a fright;
For they are so draggl'd and wet to the skin,
They're much to be pity'd, their clothing's so thin.
    Oh! Poor creatures, &c.

In case of this weather, let there be no flaw,
Take care to provide them with plenty of straw,
That when the poor wretches retire to their nest,
They may lie in comfort, and all take their rest.
  Oh! Poor hoppers, &c.

But, above all that's said, pray don't cheat the King;
For if you do that, it is sure a sad thing:
As he'll have his duty by hook or by crook!
Beware, oh! Beware, lest you're in the black book.
  Oh! Sad doings! &c.

Tho' ye have more honour, at least so I trust,
(I'd have ye be always quite upright and just,)
For honour and honesty carries the sway,
Then from these great maxims ne'er venture to stray.
  Oh! Rare hopping! &c.

So here ends my theme, for I've no more to say,
Only wish that each guest will attend to my lay,
For, faith, no exceptions are meant in my song,
And them that cries yes … by my soul, they are wrong.
  Geho Dobbin, &c.

William Cobbett (1762–1835)

Rural Rides (1822–26)

Described by Carlyle as 'the pattern John Bull of his century', William Cobbett rose from humble origins to become a Member of Parliament, farmer, economist and political reformer. He championed the working classes and was imprisoned in 1804 for two years for his attack on flogging in the army.

Rural Rides, Cobbett's most famous work, is an investigative survey of English agriculture in the depression which followed the Napoleonic Wars. Cobbett proves a shrewd, knowledgeable and practical observer, well able to communicate with all classes of society and to report his findings in an informed, clear and forthright style.

A fine investigator, he is a yardstick for the agricultural conditions of the times and his book contains a euphoric celebration of the hopping country just to the north of the Medway Valley between Maidstone and Tonbridge. Cobbett also spotted an ash plantation used for hop poles.

❧❧❧

From *Rural Rides:*

A friend at Tenterden told me that, if I had a mind to know Kent, I must go through Romney Marsh to Dover, from Dover to Sandwich, from Sandwich to Margate, from Margate to Canterbury, from Canterbury to Faversham, from Faversham to Maidstone, and from Maidstone to Tonbridge. I found from Mr Waller, this morning, that the regular turnpike route, from his house to Maidstone, was through Sittingbourne. I had been along that road several times; and besides, to be covered with dust was what I could not think of, when I had it in my power to get to Maidstone without it. I took the road across the country, quitting the London road, or rather, crossing it, in the dell, between Osprige and Green-street. I instantly began to go up hill, slowly, indeed; but up hill. I came through the villages of Newnham, Doddington, Ringlestone, and to that of Hollingbourne. I had come up hill for *thirteen miles*, from Mr Waller's house. At last, I got to the top of this hill, and went along, for some distance, upon level ground. I found I was gone upon just the same sort of land as that on the hill at Folkestone, at Reigate, at Ropley and at Ashmansworth. The red clayey loam, mixed up with great yellow flint stones. I found *fine meadows* here, just such as are at Ashmansworth (that is to say, on the north Hampshire hills). This sort of ground is characterized by an astonishing depth that they have to go for their water. At Ashmansworth, they go to a depth of more than *three hundred feet*. As I was riding along the top of this hill in Kent, I saw the same beautiful sort of meadows that there are at Ashmansworth; I saw the corn backward; I was just thinking to go up to some house, to ask how far they had to go for water, when I saw a large well-bucket, and all the chains and wheels belonging to such a concern; but here was also the tackle for a *horse* to work in drawing up the water! I asked about the depth of the well and the information I received must have been incorrect; because I was told it was three hundred yards. I asked this of a public-house keeper further on, not seeing anybody where the farmhouse was. I make no doubt that the depth is, as near as possible, that of Ashmansworth. Upon the top of this hill, I saw the finest field of beans that I have seen this year, and, by very far, indeed, the *finest piece of hops*. A beautiful piece of hops, surrounded by beautiful plantations of young ash, producing poles for hop-gardens. My road here pointed towards the West. It soon wheeled round towards the South; and, all of a sudden, I found myself upon the edge of a hill, as lofty and as steep as that of Folkestone, at Reigate, or at Ashmansworth. It was the same famous chalk-ridge that I was crossing again. When I got to the edge of the hill, and before I got off my horse to lead him down this more than mile of hill, I sat and surveyed the prospect before me, and to the right and to the left. This is what the people of Kent call the *Garden of Eden*. It is a district of meadows, corn fields, hop-gardens, and orchards of apples, pears, cherries and filberts, with very little if any land which cannot, with propriety, be called good. There are plantations of Chestnut and of Ash frequently occurring; and as these are cut when long enough to make poles for hops, they are at all times objects of great beauty.

At the foot of the hill of which I have been speaking, is the village of Hollingbourne; thence you come on to Maidstone. From Maidstone to this place (Merryworth) is about seven miles, and these are the finest seven miles that I have ever seen in England or anywhere else. The Medway is to your left, with its meadows about a mile wide. You cross the Medway, in coming out of Maidstone, and it goes and finds its way down to Rochester, through a break in the chalk-ridge. From Maidstone to Merryworth, I should think that there were hop-gardens on one half of the way on both sides of the road. Then looking across the Medway, you see hop-gardens and orchards two miles deep, on the side of a gently rising ground: and this continues with you all the way from Maidstone to Merryworth. The orchards form a great feature of the country; and the plantations of Ashes and of Chestnuts that I mentioned before, add greatly to the beauty. These gardens of hops are kept very clean, in general, though some of them have been neglected this year owing to the bad appearance of the crop.

The culture is sometimes mixed: that is to say, apple-trees or cherry-trees or filbert-trees and hops, in the same ground. This is a good way, they say, of raising an orchard. I do not believe it; and I think that nothing is gained by any of these mixtures. They plant apple-trees or cherry-trees in rows here; they then plant a filbert-tree close to each of these large fruit-trees; and then they cultivate the middle of the ground by planting potatoes. This is being too greedy. It is impossible that they can gain by this. What they gain one way they lose the other way; and I verily believe, that the most profitable way would be, never to mix things at all. In coming from Maidstone I passed through a village called Teston, where Lord Barham has a seat.

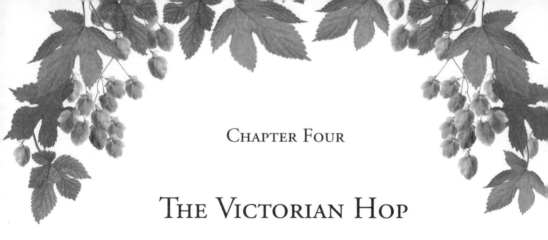

CHAPTER FOUR

THE VICTORIAN HOP

William Moy Thomas (1828–1910)

'Hops' from *Household Words* (1852)

In 1850 Charles Dickens started Household Words, *an immensely successful weekly journal of about 20,000 words, for which he planned and commissioned articles and in which he serialised new novels including his own. No article was published*

Donkey cart. (Fran & Geoff Doel Collection)

without his approval and no contributor ever had his name appended to his work, Dickens' name alone appearing on the title page. The aim was always to entertain as well as instruct.

One contributor whose written work Dickens much respected was William Moy Thomas and this, Thomas's article on Kent hops which appeared in the 16 October edition in 1852, Dickens considered 'extremely well done'. Moy Thomas was drama critic for the Daily News *and the first editor of* Cassell's Magazine. *He also wrote novels and short stories and became private secretary to Sir Charles Wentworth, proprietor of the* Athenaeum *and* Notes and Queries.

❧❧❧

Hops

Loitering upon the old stone bridge over the Medway, in the town of Maidstone, early in a misty autumn morning, I miss the ancient church and row of poplars, which I know should be somewhere near upon the left. It is of no use looking. They will not come out of their white shroud until noon; and if then, perhaps, only to enfold themselves in it again an hour or two after. The water flows on, smooth and noiseless, till it splits upon the sharp wedges of the piers, and runs away whispering under the arches; but beyond this, not a ghost of a noise is abroad. All Maidstone is asleep, except a railway porter, a man driving a cow who went over the bridge a minute or two ago, and myself. There may be somebody up at the baths behind me: I cannot see. But the old, bruised, and battered coal-barge, moored alongside the wharf, in which I believe live a man and his wife, seems to have nobody aboard – for no smoke ascends from the stove-pipe at the helm. Slowly creeping down this way – a thin ghost at first, then a dusky spectre, then a green and yellow barge – comes the *Sara Ann*, of Aylesford. Down drops the huge tawny mainsail as she steers for the middle arch, just above which I am standing, leaning cross-armed upon the parapet: and now, with all her wings close folded, she shaves to a nicety the sides of the arch. She is gone: but what is this rich odour she has left behind? Not spikenard nor olibanum could be more grateful to my nostrils, than that rich, balmy, healthful, bitter smell that floats about me now, and makes this place no common bridge of stone. The *Sarah Ann* is freighted with Kentish hops: many a precious pocket of that noble plant lies down in the dark, beneath a yellow tarpaulin spread over her hatchway. But, like the thoughts of a good man, who suffers imprisonment for the whole world's sake, its subtle essence steals abroad, and lives in the free air.

Hops coming into my head in this manner, remind me of the business of to-day: for though I have the air of a veritable lounger, and though the overtasked railway porter, going to his work at this early hour, looked at me enviously and thought I lead a nice lazy life of it, I, too, have a task to accomplish. The railway porter, if he knew anything of signals off the line, might have known that to be astir thus early does not mean idling. I have a letter in my pocket for Mr Day, the hop-grower of East Farleigh, charging him, in the sacred name of friendship, to show and make clear to me everything connected with the cultivation and preparation of hops. So ... I come to the bridge again, and cross the river winding through the brown and yellow woods up to East Farleigh.

There are in all England some fifty or sixty thousand acres of hop plantations; and of those one-half at least are in this county alone. In the oldest book I know about hops (Reynolde Scot's *Perfect Platforme of a Hoppe Garden*), dated 1574, and printed in black letter, with many prefaces terminating in inverted pyramids of type, Kent is spoken of as *the* county of hops. The system of cultivation appears to have little changed since then; and the book, if it were not written in the style of an Act of Parliament, and interlarded with moral reflections and allusions to every poet and orator of ancient times, might have been written in the present day. Yet hops, at that date, were but of recent cultivation. For ages, while our ancestors were wont to flavour their ale with ground ivy, and honey, and various bitters, a weed called 'hop' had been known about the hedges of England; but no one thought to cultivate it for brewing until the beginning of the sixteenth century. Some say the cultivated plant came first from Flanders, where it was certainly used before our brewers knew its virtues. The Chinese, of course, are supposed to have known all about it ages before that. In France, hop gardens are very ancient. Mention is made of them in some of the oldest records, though what their hops were used for does not appear. In England it had many enemies to contend with at first. Slanderers said it dried up the body and increased melancholy; and though the very reverse is the fact, this belief so far prevailed, that we find in the household regulations of Henry the Eighth an order to the brewer not to put any more hops in the beer: and at a much later period, the Common Council of the City of London petitioned Parliament against the use of hops, 'in regard that they would spoil the taste of the drink, and endanger the people.'

There are not five parishes in Kent – large or small – that have so many acres of hops as this little parish of East Farleigh, where I am going. There is no place in all England whose hops will fetch a better price ... At East Farleigh dwelt the Rothschild of hop-growers, whose hop-poles alone were said to be worth seventy thousand pounds; ... The luxuriance of hops about here is a puzzle to theoretical agriculturalists. 'Though rich mould,' says Bannister, 'generally produces a larger growth of hops than other soils, there is *one* exception to this rule, where the growth is frequently eighteen or twenty hundred per acre.' This is the neighbourhood of Maidstone, a kind of slaty ground with an understratum of stone. There the vines run up to the top of the longest poles, and the increase is equal to the most fertile soil of any kind.

Hops, in England, invariably grow up poles. In the north of France they are sometimes made to creep upon copper wires, ranged horizontally, like the lines of the electric telegraph; but Kentish farmers, when they hear of it, shake their heads. These poles stand in groups of three or four, at a distance of about six or seven feet apart; and nearly three thousand (worth about seventy-five pounds) are required for an acre of ground. In some counties, hops are set between fruit-trees in orchards; and penny wise and pound foolish growers will plant vegetables between the poles; but Kentish growers know that the hop requires all the strength of the soil, and rigidly exclude everything that could impoverish it, except in the first two years after planting, when the bines never produce any flowers worth picking. The only plant cultivated is the female hop; the male species, sometimes called 'blind hop' being of no value: though it is said that if the male hop were excluded from the garden, the flowers throughout the ground would be wanting in that yellow powder called the 'farina', or 'condition', which is their chief virtue. For this reason, one male hop plant in every hundred groups is generally planted. Of the hop cultivated there are eight or ten varieties, of which that called 'Goldings' is the best; but this, from its very luxuriance, is subject to diseases which poorer but more hardy kinds will escape. Some of each sort are, therefore, generally planted.

... Its flowers [are] known to be a powerful soporific. A pillow of hops, recommended for George the Third, in his illness of 1787, was found to produce sleep when all other means had failed.

... Emerging from the woods, just as the mists are creeping away ... I see nothing but hops on each side of the river. All up the sides of the valley, their heavy clusters, topping the high poles, peep one over the other, like spectators' heads in the pit of a theatre. And now I spy the stone bridge with its four pointed arches ... And there, a few yards above the bridge, struggling for a place among the hop grounds, stands the old church of East Farleigh, like three barns with a pointed spire. And here I stop, and leave the river to wind away and hide itself in a perfect forest of hop plantations.

While my host runs his eye along the lines of my letter, I read in his face that the sacred name of friendship will not have been invoked in vain. He does not think of hinting that Saturday is a busy day; but on the contrary congratulates me upon having chosen that day, as presenting some features in hop picking not to be seen on any other. So we walk together through the hop-garden, where the strong bitter odour and the bright yellow of the clusters, tell that they are ripe, till we come to a stubble field, and find the pickers at work upon the borders of the plantation. Men, women, and children all pick hops. This is why this employment is preferred by those wandering bands who cut hay in the spring and corn in the summer, and in the winter live, or die, no one knows where. But these are by no means the only class that comes hopping. Labourers, costermongers, factory girls, skirt-makers, fishermen's boys, jolly young watermen, and they tell me, even clerks out of employment, all throng the Kentish highways at this time, attracted by the opportunity of earning a couple of shillings per day; and still the cry is more, and the farmer, in plentiful seasons, is frequently embarrassed for want of hands.

… The man who, with his instrument – which he calls a hop-dog, because it is a hook on one side and a knife on the other … cuts the bine about the roots, and then hooks up pole, bine, and all, and lays it across the pickers' bins, has enough to do to keep ten pickers supplied. A sullen-looking girl … grumbles at being kept waiting for a moment. So does another young woman, who has brought her infant family with her in a covered child's wagon – egged on by a surly murmur from a wild young man, with white hair and eyebrows … Meanwhile the cutter makes a desperate attack upon the poles; felling them so fast that he has time to pull out a handkerchief and rub the perspiration from his forehead; and the surly young woman admits that 'he is keepin' the pot a-bilin': and now every-body is busy. Down comes a hop-pole, and away goes a swift hand up it, plucking the flowers into a canvas bin upon a wooden frame, carefully avoiding the leaves till it gets near the top of the pole, when with one stroke it rubs off all that remain, the few little green leaves at top doing no harm. The pole, with the bine stripped of its flowers, is then thrown aside, just as the cutter, who has served eight or nine in the interval, drops another pole across the bin. Each but these bins, I am told, holds fifteen or twenty bushels, which is as much as the fastest hand can pick in a day. The lower parts of the poles – which are rotted by being in the earth – are then cut away, and the poles will be carefully stacked to serve for shorter plants next year.

Here are the oast-houses – most of them brick-built and perfectly circular up to a height of fourteen or fifteen feet, whence they terminate in a cone, surmounted by a cowled chimney, peculiarly shaped, to allow the vapour from the hops to escape ... Some of the oast-houses are square – but that shape is old-fashioned – and some are long: for no two farmers agree in any one particular as to the treatment of hops. Even as to furnaces opinions are so diverse, and are supported by such well-balanced testimony, that I find all kinds of stoves here. Entering at a narrow aperture, and darting past the fire, through a heat that would roast me if I stood still in it, I find myself in a circular chamber about eighteen feet in diameter. In the midst, or rather, nearer to the aperture, a clear fire of coke and charcoal burns with thin hovering flames, melting into air. Dipping his hand into a barrel, my conductor brings up some rolls of brimstone; and, casting them on the fire, a bright blue glare lights up the chamber and the faces of all present. This is found to give a livelier colour to the hops, and is everywhere, except at Farnham, adopted: colour – although it is said to be not really a sign of strength – being arbitrarily insisted on by the purchaser ... With a slightly disagreeable taste in the throat, I escape into the next oast-house. Here the fire is enclosed in a sort of oven, quite hidden from sight. In another, I find it in a brick stove with apertures for the escape of heat, contrived by omitting a brick here and there. These apertures are called 'horses'; but, like the bine-cutter's 'hop-dog', the origin of the name is involved in obscurity. Here is a different kind of stove, in which the fire is closely shut up, and the heated air is confined and carried up to the drying-floor by an inverted hollow cone, formed of laths and clay, and lined inside with smooth tiles.

Walking out into the open air again, we mount a ladder to the cooling-room attached to the oast-house. On a circular floor, about fifty-six feet in circumference, formed of strong wire netting and covered with coarse hair cloth, through which the warm air ascends, the hop-flowers lie to a depth of two or three feet. One thousand and fifty pounds' weight of green hops are here drying at once; but through the little aperture at the top of this sugar-loaf chamber, some eight hundred and fifty pounds of this weight will evaporate into air, so that a day's work of the fastest picker, weighing a hundred pounds when green, will scarcely weigh twenty when dry. The air is only moderately warm; but the grower, by long experience (for nothing else will make a hop-drier), knows without any thermometer that it is exactly the proper heat – considering the weather, the state of the hops, and a dozen other things. The drying never ceases during the time of picking, and is one of the most difficult branches of the preparation. A man must watch them day and night, turning them frequently, until the stalks look shrivelled, and burying his arms deep in the hops, he feels them to be dry. This is generally after eight or twelve hours' drying, after which they are shovelled through the little door on to the adjoining cooling-floor to make room for more.

On the cooling-floor I find a man stitching hop-pockets ... He is working on canvas hung over a line, with needles that would not go through any button-hole in the world ... Into these pockets the hops are tightly wedged; and – dusted from head to foot with the yellow powder of the hops – a man in a blouse (which used to be blue before hopping began) is continually passing to and fro, wheeling a single pocket at a time upon a long truck, from the steps of the cooling loft to a pair of great scales in an open shed. Here stands the supervisor, the representative of Her Majesty's Board of Inland Revenue. He is a very stout, red-faced man, with a white hat, and a brown velvet shooting-jacket, and carries a small bunch of hops in his mouth. He holds a book in his hand full of lines and figures, red and black, and looks very cross; as one who, by the stern expression of his features, would warn off all attempts at bribery of any kind. Not so his lean, but equally red-faced assistant. Though, perhaps, not less incorruptible because he twits the farmer with making his fortune out of hops, and calls himself a poor devil ... He generally comes alone, but now and then, as a check upon him, the stout superior drops in unexpectedly, and re-weighs what he has booked. One by one, the great pockets are rolled into the scale and rolled out again, and laid all in a row like bloated porpoises – the handles at the corners being the two short sprawling fins. Then my conductor ... bestrides one of the porpoises, like a merry merman under the sea and with a basin of ink in one hand, and a small painting brush in the other, cries out, 'Number!' The supervisor refers to his book, and answers, 'One hundred and fifty'; and those three figures are drawn upon the animal's back, a little above the snout. 'Weight!' 'One, two, twelve.' Down goes one hundredweight, two quarters, twelve pounds. Next, in letters four inches long (according to the statute), he adds his own name and parish, and the date, with an indignant allusion to an act intended to be passed last session; which, abolishing this part of the ceremony, would have robbed Farleigh hops of their glory in the market ... Finally, the supervisor (checking the figures) takes the brush and marks a cross upon the seam of the mouth of the sack, to prevent frauds on the Government by afterwards squeezing in more hops. This is called 'sealing', which being done, he closes his book with the intention of calling in six months' time for a duty of one penny and twelve twentieths of a farthing per pound weight.

... Not yet, however, is the grower sure of his profit. The hops may remain on his hands for a twelvemonth, when they will be considered as 'old hops', and lose much in value. Nor can the abundance of one season find a balance in the deficiency of others. In a year or two, if kept, they will be worthless – as odourless and flavourless as mere chaff ... Woe betide the man who, with too small a capital to carry him over reverses, sets up as a hop-planter!

... We have something else to see. The pickers are waiting to be paid in the hop garden; for it is Saturday night. Our shadows are strangely angular and gawky as we walk along the stubble field again; the pickers leave off before sunset, to allow time for carrying away the hops by daylight. Their work has to be measured first. The cutter leaves off battling with the rows of poles, and comes to measure with a wicker bushel having a black line round it, outside about half way up. For any one of these bushels, filled as lightly as possible – never quite up to the top – the picker receives twopence. When only a few hops remain at the bottom of the bin, he watches most anxiously; for if the remainder reaches beyond the black line it counts a bushel: while if it falls short, it counts as nothing. There is a delay at the sullen-looking girl's bin, for she has dropped in too many leaves, and must pick them out, one by one. Cutter 'wonders she didn't put in bines, poles and all,' and bids her 'look alive'. When everything is done, the farmer brings his money bag, attended by a boy, who reads the amounts to be paid from a book. Most of the hands have been drawing money in the week – they don't know how much exactly, nor when, but the book assists their memories. Nobody can recollect, either, how much he has earned, but contents himself when he is informed by saying, he 'thought it was ever so much more,' by way of showing that he is on the alert, and not to be cheated easily. The merry old woman takes her money gaily. Sullen girl grumbles. Eager faces are crowded around the payer. There is a man with a very savage heavy look, which has been all along fixed intently upon the money bag. 'How much you?'

'Oh! You know.' Book is referred to and the savage man pounces upon fifteen shillings. 'Now, then; is everybody paid?' There is a tidy, quiet, freckle-faced girl standing a little way off, whom the merry old woman spies, and says to her, 'Why didn't you go up?' The girl says, 'I didn't like to ask for it.' On this the merry old woman drags her up to the farmer, and she, too, is paid. The pokes are wheeled off; and the cutter drains the great stone beer bottle; and the merry old woman encumbers herself with many bundles and two umbrellas; and all go talking and laughing across the field, followed by the woman drawing her infant family in the covered child's wagon.

There is a great stir and a strange noise of voices over East Farleigh to-night. In this little out-of-the-way village of some twenty houses scattered about, and with only one beer-shop, three thousand hop-pickers (chiefly Irish) are assembled. Hundreds of fires in the open air look from a distance like the encampment of an army. In huts and stables and outhouses; in abandoned mills; in crumbling barns and dilapidated oast-houses whose cracks are ineffectually stuffed with straw and clay; under pents; against walls; in tents and under canvas awnings, this multitude cook, eat, drink, smoke and sleep. No wonder that in the ground of the old church, I find a row of grass-grown mounds, with an inscription on wood, 'In memory of forty-three strangers, who died September, 1849. R.I.P.' A parishioner tells me they were all Irish hoppers; and only a portion of those who died of cholera here in the season of that year. No inhabitant of the parish was attacked; and to the credit of the clergyman it is said that he turned his house into a temporary hospital, and with his wife attended them night and day.

At the bridge, some are washing clothes: women and girls and boys, wild, ragged, uncouth wretches, most of them standing bare-legged in the water rinsing shirts in saucepans, and dabbing them against the smutty edges as fast as they are cleaned; boiling other clothes in cauldrons; and hanging garments that have more superficies of hole than cotton, upon the hedges. There, too, are hideous old Sycoraxes smoking and crouching over fires this warm day, and shouting unintelligible sounds to fat children, sprawling in the mud upon the shelving bank of the river. Everybody has been paid to-night, and most are off to buy provisions for the week. There is a solitary butcher's shop up the lane, with trees in front, which is besieged. All round it – for it is open on three sides – a hungry mob hustle and push and clamour to be served; and the butcher, who all the year round has not a whole sheep in his shop, now chops his way out of heaps of meat. Then there is a lonely grocer's – lonely no more – where as great a crowd clamours for bacon, and bread, and beer, and tea, and sugar, in a great gloomy shop lit by two wretched candles. The only beer-shop overflows with disappointed customers, and the wild howl of Irish singers. Hundreds are encamped at the cross-road. Here is a double row of huts, built expressly for the hoppers, each about ten feet square, with a shelving roof, where half-a-dozen men, women, and girls sleep together upon straw, and have a fire. There are bread stalls, and stalls of herrings in brine, and stalls of such pastry as I never beheld before. One of the huts is open on one side, and converted into a shop or stall, where you may buy bread, and candles, and such small quantities of tea and sugar, all ready done up in paper, as never were sold at any other time or place. This is the private speculation of Mr Bleary, who is encouraged by the great hop-growers to sell provisions here at this time; they having a good opinion of his mode of doing business.

Mr Bleary is said to be a man of property, and I am introduced to him. He is a very stout Irishman, with a moist eye, and a treble chin lapping over a white cravat, and has a chronic cold in the head: calls himself 'Purvey-her in gin'ral to the strangers in Farrerleigh;'... He ... bids me follow him into his hut, or shop; and describes an arbitrary division of its only room into kitchen, parlour, and bed-room. 'The furrerniture isn't all come down yet; but no matter.' Mr Bleary is full of anecdotes, with wrathful parentheses of 'disorderly doins, and shemful robbin' of poor creeturs' by his predecessors in the "purveyhership".' But, coming forth and seeing his lines of customers, all sitting at long tables, drinking soup in the light of the moon, the poetry of his whole being overflows:

'Look at me happy children! All livin' in harrermony one with another: all drinkin' soup and bread, and discoorsin' together, like ladies and gentlemen, about politics and the late Juke o' Willington. Look at me happy children! You remember how it used to be, Misther Day? How they used to fight like as many wolves, and lie about the ground like a flock o' pigs. There's soup for a half-penny a basin! Taste it. Here I stand in defiance of all dochors. Let 'em all come down to East Farrerleigh and examine it. Oh, the days before I came down here! I remember 'em well. What shindies! There usen't to be never a sound head, nor a sound winder in all East Farrerleigh parish. And only look at 'em now. Ask 'em themselves if they don't feel morer like Christians, and a little morer happy-minded.'

And thus Mr Bleary continues till he bids me good night ... Good night, Mr Bleary! My road lies Maidstone way, beside the river shining in the full moon: and I would for your sake, I had started an hour earlier. Then should I not have been compelled to tell how wild disorder broke out in that happy family, that night; how sticks and stockings loaded with Mr Bleary's stones were flourished, and heads and windows broken, just as in the days of old. How drunken hoppers sprawled about as if you had never come to East Farleigh, and had never sold sugar there, nor soup; and how your mild paternal admonitions were laughed to scorn.

Fran & Geoff Doel

Transport, Accommodation & Traditions

In the nineteenth and early twentieth centuries beer consumption in England was huge and led to thousands of acres in Kent being turned over to hops. The Kentish farmers were now reliant on a casual workforce from London, most of them coming from poor housing. At first the pickers made their way to the Kentish hop-gardens in coster-barrows and pony carts though the very poorest

Hopper Special. (Fran & Geoff Doel Collection)

were prepared to walk 20 or 30 miles into the heart of Kent, often starting their journey along the Old Kent Road and sleeping overnight in hedges. A bed for the night could also be got in some of the workhouse dormitories while some farmers permitted pickers en route to sleep in their barns.

When the railway network expanded in the nineteenth century the Southern Railway decided to provide subsidised trains called 'Hoppers' Specials' for London pickers. The first trains appeared in 1876 and ran through the night, the passengers initially and perhaps humiliatingly packed into cattle trucks. Old running stock was then used. After a slow journey the pickers were usually dropped off at first light. Some Victorian families could be very large and it was a well-known secret that many hopping families could not afford to buy train tickets for all their children. Legendary stories claim that children were secreted under their mother's, or their auntie's or grannie's voluminous long skirts; sometimes they were hidden at the bottom of the massive old pram or box on wheels which hoppers used to transport their goods to the hop farms; the latter was normally full of heaped-up clothes and bedclothes, household items and tins of food, sometimes even the family canary in its cage. Farmers sent horses and carts (later lorries) to meet the pickers in the early hours of the morning and the families were conveyed to the various hop farms where they were allocated their accommodation. 'The Specials' likewise brought visitors (usually husbands) down to the fields at the weekend. In 1925 the book *Working-class Organisations and Popular Tourism, 1840–1970* told us that seventy-one 'hoppers Specials were run by the Southern Railway into Kent and seventy-five back out. They carried 34,448 hoppers and 39,950 friends on Saturday, with another 13,850 on Sundays. Even in 1945 sixty special trains brought 30,000 hop-pickers to Kent.'

The same source tells us that:

Those who have memories of hopping in its last phase in the fifties and sixties know that the Cockneys welcomed the opportunity to go hop picking which they regarded as an enjoyable six week working-holiday in the Kent countryside; on the downward journey they would often sing 'all the way' usually to concertina and accordion accompaniments.

One ex-picker claimed:

Hop-picking was our holiday. It was brilliant to get away from where we lived. But, mind you, it was bloody hard down there, in the hop-fields, but it was better down there because we had the open air. We used to play a game of football, or play cricket on Sundays in the fields. There were plenty of open spaces.

However, there were many who agreed with George Orwell that 'It is because hopping is regarded as a holiday that the pickers will take such starvation wages.' He considered the farmers to be exploitative, because they regarded Londoners as cheap labour and accordingly paid the workforce badly for their efforts.

Accommodation for the hoppers

Orwell, writing in the '30s, recorded that the hut to which he had been allocated was 10ft across with no glass in the window and with a number of holes that let in the wind and the rain. The bed, provided by the farmer, was only a heap of straw and hop bines; for cooking and heating there was some firewood placed outside the hut but the only toilet was so far away and so filthy he could not bear to use it and the water supply consisted of only one communal water tap.

By the 1950s the pickers still had outside fires but they did have a provision of chemical toilets and electric lighting, and picnic tables 'so that the workers need not eat on the ground'.

Being so jam-packed, inevitably lice and nits were prevalent and contagious illnesses could spread like wildfire as when, in September 1848, an outbreak of cholera killed forty-three hop pickers in East Farleigh and in 1897, the year Father Richard Wilson opened his Little Hoppers Hospital at Five Oak Green, there was an outbreak of smallpox. Some farmers acquired ex-army tents for their workforce but in 1874 new bye-laws were brought in under the Sanitary Amendment Act regarding hoppers' accommodation and purpose-built hoppers' huts was the result.

This is a late nineteenth-century account of the huts:

The huts for the use of the hoppers stand in rows of eight houses; with a cook and wash-house in the middle; and are divided into eight compartments, each about 12 feet square. One company, numbering (up to) ten persons, is assigned to each compartment. The floor is thickly littered with straw for sleeping, but no chairs, forms or tables are provided. Hanging on an iron nail in the wall is an old lantern, in which the Hopper burns a candle. Washing conveniences are found by the Hoppers, and in many instances they bring bedding with them to lay over the straw … The cook and wash-house is usually in the centre of each row of huts. The front is open to the air; and there are three or four fireplaces … The farmer finds the Hoppers faggots for burning; affixes hooks on which to hang the kettles, and six pots can hang at one time over the fires. The huts are built with bricks, roofed with tiles and one storey in height … the washing … is done in the open air, and the hedges, or the grass, utilised for drying purposes.

The following 'general regulations' drawn up to be exhibited in the nineteenth-century hop-gardens reminds us that cigarette smoking was common and always considered a fire-risk by the farmer:

General Regulations
No lucifer matches to be used within the distance of five hills from a bin;
No smoking allowed near the buildings or premises;
No fire or light to be used after nine o'clock in the evening except on Saturdays, and no smoking allowed after that hour;
No spirituous liquors to be sold or bought in the hop-gardens;

No abusive, improper or immoral language to be made use of;
No quarreling or fighting to take place.
For any breach of these general orders, the person offending shall forfeit one shilling.

Some Kent publicans did not permit the hoppers to drink inside their pubs. After being served, the hoppers took their beer outside. There they congregated in groups, sometimes around a musician playing a concertina or melodeon, sometimes round a fire, and 'there would be some step-dancing in couples or singly and a lot of singing'. As Moy Thomas recounts in the previous article, an excess of drinking at the weekends often led to bad language and unsocial fracas amongst the hoppers and explains why so many of the Kent villagers during the hopping season took elaborate precautions to protect their property and stock and why many of the pubs were unwelcoming. During the late Victorian period the temperance movement took the opportunity to target hoppers in the field but this was not always well received by the hoppers.

'Queen hops', 'The Old Man', and the hop-pillow

Finding a 'Queen hop' (a rather rare, extra-large hop) on the bine was equivalent to finding a four-leafed clover, and viewed by pickers as a luck-bringer. But the greatest of good luck was obtained from 'The Old Man', the last vine to be picked in each hop-garden. Another firmly held belief which had existed in earlier times was in the efficacy of a hop-pillow (a small cushion stuffed with hop cones) which was claimed to induce sleep and was thought to help cure headaches and migraine.

John B. Marsh (1835–1902)

From *Hops & Hopping* (1892)

The Hoppers live upon fish, tinned meat, and German sausages during the week; and upon Sunday have a joint bedded upon potatoes roasted at the local oven. About the hour for going to church the Hoppers may be met carrying their baking tins to the oven; and scarcely less than from seventy to one hundred tins are received at the baker's on the Sunday morning. Fetching the joint home is a matter of much ceremony; and no single man or woman is entrusted with the sole care of the tin, there is always an escort to relieve the carrier, and generally to ensure the safety of the dinner. During sermon time, the women finish up their clothes washing, wringing, and drying – the grass and the hedges are littered with the garments of the poor people; and the youths and men either bathe, with a great deal of unnecessary shouting, or try their hand at fishing. As there are no tables in the huts, the tin of food is placed on the ground, and the family squat around. The mother or father cuts the joint with any sort of cutting tool which is handy, frequently a pocket knife, and the hungry workers help themselves out of the dish with anything capable of spitting a potato, or holding it while being devoured. The utility of fingers comes into admirable display on these occasions. After dinner the men smoke, or visit; the women gossip; and the children play. As soon as the public-houses are open, there is a general migration in their direction, and drinking and singing proceed until closing time. But the beershops are now closely run by the coffee-houses, where wholesome and well-cooked victuals are supplied; where the strangers always receive a hearty welcome; and where ladies and gentlemen without any air of superiority mingle with the people, advise with them, and encourage them to make a stand against the terrible temptations which dog their every step. During the week nights the girls are taught to read and write; to mend their own clothes and to cook; and thus they learn to become self-reliant and hopeful for the future.

Costermongers out in Kent. (Fran & Geoff Doel Collection)

The costers of the East-end follow their customers in great numbers; and set up their stalls in the village market places, selling tinned food, joints, or knuckles of ham at low prices. They remain throughout the season; and drive a rattling trade when the harvest is a good one. Fresh supplies come down by train; and the Hoppers, who are naturally suspicious, prefer trading with these men, to dealing exclusively with little shop-keepers.

The same costermongers come down to the same villages year after year. 'Ned' is always to be found at the corner by the pub, with tinned meat; and close beside him 'Tommy' with stores of fish – bloaters, kippers, herrings; and 'Snooks' deals in bacon and cheese. Inspectors, in the service of the local authority, are constantly going round, and bad food is invariably seized. The local shopkeeper has to compete with these 'stranger merchants'; and keeps his own position well. He has this advantage over the costers; he lays in stocks of articles which the Hopper requires, and sells at low prices. Empty meat tins in which to boil potatoes are given to customers; margarine tubs for washing are sold for a penny halfpenny or tuppence each; while tin kettles which hold two gallons are retailed at from four pence to eleven pence.

As to the earnings of a Hopper, an average is hard to ascertain, on account of the variation of the seasons and the number who pick together; but it probably averages £1 a week.

The Drowning at Hartlake Bridge

Account from the *London Illustrated News* (1853)

Many gipsies today make a point of visiting the bridge at Hartlake in mid-Kent where they throw a wreath of hops into the River Medway. These are the descendants of thirty men and women who died in an accident here on 25 October 1853. Forty pickers, men, women and children, were being transported back on wagons to their hopping huts after a day's picking near the village of Hadlow when one of the horses lost its footing and the cart crashed through the rotted wood fence of the bridge and tipped the occupants into the Medway. The river was in a high state of flood and thirty were swept away and drowned. News of the deaths brought what seemed like 'all the gipsy tribes in England' to came to Hadlow. A pyramid-shaped memorial in the churchyard at Hadlow commemorates their loss along with the names of the dead hop-pickers.

The hop-pickers' memorial in Hadlow Churchyard. (Fran & Geoff Doel Collection)

John B. Marsh

'The Hartlake Bridge Disaster' from *Hops and Hopping* (1892)

There had been a flood – a most unusual occurrence at the season of the year – and some low-lying gardens, where gipsy pickers were at work, became flooded so as to hinder picking. The farmer having other gardens high and dry, resolved to transfer the Hoppers from one ground to the other. As the river Medway separated the two gardens, and the approaches to the bridge were flooded, the farmer sent a wagon drawn by two horses tandem fashion, to bring off the people. The wagon was duly loaded – there being between thirty and forty in it – and started to cross the bridge. On the fore horse rode a labourer. When they came to the river they found that the flood had risen suddenly, and the water was rushing over the level of the bridge. Not thinking of any danger, the wagon drove on to the bridge, and when half-way across, the horse in the shafts swerved a foot or two, causing the vehicle to strike the centre post of the structure. In an instant the post snapped, and the water carried the wagon over the side, capsizing as it fell. The poor gipsies had little chance of saving their lives, and thirty men, women, and young girls met a watery grave. The shafts broke as the wagon fell into the water, and the horses and driver escaped; but very few of those who were in the wagon were saved. Men who were well-known swimmers perished, along with women and

No.	When Died.	Name and Surname.	Sex.	Age.	Rank or Profession.	Cause of Death.	Signature, Description, and Residence of Informant.	When Registered.	Signature of Registrar.
396	Twentieth of October 1853 Hartlake Hadlow	Charlotte Leatherland	Female	55 years	Wife of Samuel Leatherland Labourer	Accidentally drowned	J N Dudlow Coroner West Malling	Twenty second October 1853	Wm Ware Registrar
397	Twentieth of October 1853 Hartlake Hadlow	Comfort Leatherland	Female	24 years	Daughter of Samuel Leatherland Labourer	Accidentally drowned	J N Dudlow Coroner West Malling	Twenty second October 1853	Wm Ware Registrar
398	Twentieth of October 1853 Hartlake Hadlow	James Mouser	Male	18 years	Labourer	Accidentally drowned	J N Dudlow Coroner West Malling	Twenty second October 1853	Wm Ware Registrar
399	Twentieth of October 1853 Hartlake Hadlow	Contenia Herne	Female	4 years	Daughter of John Herne Labourer	Accidentally drowned	J N Dudlow Coroner West Malling	Twenty second October 1853	Wm Ware Registrar
400	Twentieth of October 1853 Hartlake Hadlow	Kitty Roach	Female	22 years	Single woman	Accidentally drowned	J N Dudlow Coroner West Malling	Twenty second October 1853	Wm Ware Registrar

Death certificate for the Hartlake Bridge Disaster. (Fran & Geoff Doel Collection)

children; one or two were reported to have been washed into trees by the side of the river, and were rescued next day. In one case only a boy survived, while father, mother, sisters and brothers were drowned. Many days elapsed before the bodies were recovered; and great difficulty was experienced in identifying them. Those who remember seeing the bodies afterwards laid out in barns, still speak of the great beauty of the dead gipsy girls. As soon as the disaster became known, all the gipsy tribes in the country flocked to the quiet Kent village where their dead friends lay, and the mourning was accompanied with the most heartrending demonstrations of grief. The dead gipsies were buried in the churchyard of Hadlow, where, upon a square pillar, there stands a small pyramid, erected to the memory of the unfortunate people. On one side are the following words:

'This monument was erected by Public Subscription in memory of the Thirty Hop-Pickers who were drowned at Hartlake Bridge in a flood of the river Medway, on the 20th of October, 1853, and whose bodies were buried in the churchyard. In the midst of life we are in death.'

On the other sides are the following names: 'Samuel Leatherland aged 59, Charlotte Leatherland 56, Comfort Leatherland 24, Selina Leatherland 22, Alice Leatherland 18, John Herne 28, Lunia Herne 26, Centine Herne 4, Herne 2; all one family – Sarah Tayler aged 55, Thomas Tayler 38, Thomas Tayler 4, William Elsley 22, Selina Elsley 25, James Manser 18, Richard Read 30, Ann Howard 49, Selina Maria Knight 6 – Norah Donovan aged 31, Catharine Roach 21, Bridget Flinn 20, Ellen Collins 40, Mary Quinn 22, Jeremiah Murphy 50, Ellen Dwine 19, Margaret Mahoney 18, Catharine Preswell 24, Catharine Clare 28, Catharine Donhohue 42, Margaret King 20; all natives of Ireland.'

Song

'Hartlake Bridge'
(Traditional Song from the Traveller Tradition)

Mike Yates has researched the rich tradition of Traveller songs in Kent and Sussex, collecting material at the famous Yalding Horse Fair. His haul included Joe Jones singing 'John Barleycorn', Joe Cooper singing 'Ripest Apples' and Jasper Smith's version of 'The Hartlake Bridge Disaster', with its interesting corruption of 'Golders Green' for 'Golden Green' (which we have taken the liberty of amending in the version below):

Now seven and thirty strangers, Oh a-hopping they had been;
They were 'ployed by Mr Cox's only row, Golden Green
It were in the parish of Hadlow, that's near old Tonbridge Town,
But to hear the screams from those poor souls when they were going down.

Now some were men and women and the others girls and boys.
They kept in contact with the bridge till the horses they took shy.
They kept in contact with the bridge till the horses they took shy,
But to hear the screams from those poor souls as they were going down.

Now some were men and women, the others girls and boys.
They were 'ployed by Mr Cox's only row Golden Green.
It was in the parish of Hadlow, that's near old Tonbridge town,
But to hear the screams from those poor souls when they were going down.

Alice Ransom

Letter on the Hartlake Bridge Disaster of 1853 (Written 1984) Addressed to Mrs Anne Hughes

Anne Hughes came to Hadlow in 1969 with three small children. She went to the inaugural meeting of Hadlow Historical Society in 1971 and has been a member ever since, including being chairman and now secretary for many years. Her first research into local history was that of her own house, spreading gradually into the history of Hadlow and area. In 1984 the son-in-law of Alice Ransom came to Hadlow and asked for information on the Hartlake accident of 1853, when Alice's great-great-great-grandmother, Sarah Taylor, and other relatives had drowned. This eventually led to a memorial service being held to mark the 150th anniversary of the tragedy. Sadly Alice did not live to be at this service, but the moving family story she wrote was read by her sister, Annie Brazil, and recorded by Radio Kent.

❧❧❧

Dear Mrs Hughes,

What happened that black October night. My grannys grandmother and grandfather was hop-picking nr. Paddock Wood. She said she had just put her to little boys to bed; one 4 one 3. The 4 year old become my grannys father when a young gipsy lad came on horse back to tell them what had happend. He was crying so much that they could not make out what he was saying. At last he told them that thay was all drowned. He could not tell them no moor for he was in sutch a bad way. The old lady how lived in the cottage nr by told them to bring all the little gipsy children to the cottage and she would look after them while the rest of the gipsies go and find out what was going on. Some of the man rod donkeys to the seen. The woman walked. When my grannys granny got ther she was met by her Aunt Emily, her mothers youngest sister. She cradle her niece in her arms and cried bitterly. She told her niece I have lost a dear sister and you have lost your dear mother. Thay say Toms little Tom was on her lap. Hes gone to. We can't find Thomas or Nat. We think they have been drowned (Thay was her to brothers) They was to powerful swimmers, thay was allways swimming. Thay was all up at the oast house when some one come and told them that their tents was all waterloged, so that they had to go home and see what thay could save, but thay lost thier lives instead. It was terrible when thay draged ther lov ones out of the water. Grannys granny said she see her brother Thomas being draged out, she said the screams could be heard for miles. My grannys grandfther come and took hes wife from the seen because she was with child. She was 4 months gon. The traveling people was coming from all over the place (for news travels fast amongst the Romany race) They comfort each other. Thay got all the little children together for ther was some little children how lost mothers fathers sisters and brothers. Relatives how come from afar trying to comfort the little ones. My grannys granny said ther was one little boy who never had no one. The only one he had was hes mother and she was drowed so he was left in the world all alone. Hes mothers boddy was hooked up by some old tree stumps and he was on top of her but he never new hes mother was under him untill he was pulled out. She saved his life. He sat on her coffin all the way to the burial. The gipsy said the farmer took the little boy. I dont no if that was right and some said the gipsies took him. … The people of Hadlow and the nr. by villages was wonderful to them and my grannys granny never forgot them. The gipsies would come back every year to the memorial.

Hop-pickers on wagons. (Fran & Geoff Doel Collection)

Anne Hughes

The Hop-Pickers' Memorial Service, 19 October 2003, St Mary's Church, Hadlow

Earlier this year when I realised it would be the 150th anniversary of the Hartlake accident I asked our new vicar, the Rev. Gwen Smith, if she would be willing to hold a memorial service. We envisaged a small, informal service with local people and descendants of the thirty victims coming together to remember those who lost their lives. Neither of us guessed how much interest there would be in the event. Jo Burn of Radio Kent's 'Voices' came to Hadlow to find out about the accident and see the memorial. A few weeks later she asked if Radio Kent could record the service, so the Diocese had to be consulted. Luckily they were agreeable, but this meant more people becoming involved. After many phone calls and consultations, the order of service evolved, partly based on the Iona form of worship. Radio Kent decided to broadcast live over two hours. Local press and television became interested, with some interviews taking place at short notice. We had to make arrangements for car parking but had no idea how many would actually turn up. Members of St Mary's Church were asked to provide home-made cakes for refreshments. The organist, choir and bell-ringers agreed to take part. Marcia Wright spent about four hours cleaning the memorial and others tidied up the churchyard. My husband and Roger Stanley prepared information boards.

Luckily the weather was kind on the 19th October. Bill and I greeted visitors as they arrived and handed our service sheets, while the churchwardens showed people to their seats. There were at least thirty descendants of the victims, most related to the Taylor family. Janet and Sharon represented the Society, together with their partners. There were members of the Gypsy Council, Thomas Acton from Greenwich University and the Mayor of Tonbridge and Malling, Jill Anderson of Hadlow and her escort, together with many Hadlow residents, the total congregation amounting to about 200 people.

The Rev. Gwen welcomed everyone and the service began with 'Abide with me'. Following a reading from Revelation 22, an address was given by a visiting chaplain. I must admit I was somewhat upset to hear him refer to prejudice and felt this inappropriate when so many people had worked hard to make the service a memorable occasion. A recording was then played of Anne Brazil reading moving extracts from her sister Alice Ransom's account of the family story – they are direct descendants of Sarah Taylor who died alongside her son and grandson. After prayers, a candle was lit for each of the victims as they were remembered by name. The hymn 'The day thou gavest, Lord, is ended' was followed by a reading of the Lord's Prayer in Romany, then the congregation joined in the traditional version. The final hymn 'One more step along the world I go' had been suggested by Janet. The service ended with an Irish blessing – some of the victims of the accident were Irish.

As the bells rang out, flowers were placed at the foot of the memorial by the Gypsy Council, the Taylor and Brazil families, together with a hop wreath from Radio Kent, while the traditional song 'Hartlake Bridge' was sung by Ambrose Cooper. Visitors and local residents were then able to chat together over tea and cakes.

Since the service both Gwen and I have received several messages of appreciation both from people who were in the church and those who heard it on Radio Kent. I was particularly pleased to hear from a lady whose great-grandmother had been saved from drowning and eventually lived to be 100!

Song

'The Irish Hop Pole Puller' (Traditional Folk Song from the Singing of George 'Pop' Maynard of Copthorne (1872–1962))

This amusing song of a London laundry girl who deserts her coster boyfriend to run off with an Irish hop-pole puller was collected and recorded by Ken Stubbs from the

George 'Pop' Maynard, the famous traditional singer, playing marbles. (Fran & Geoff Doel Collection)

singing of George 'Pop' Maynard from Copthorne in Sussex, who annually went hop picking in Kent.

'Pop' was one of the finest of the southern traditional singers, with a magnificent voice and repertoire, who continued singing at his local pub, The Cherry Tree, until shortly before his death at the age of 90. George was also a champion marbles player at the nearby Tinsley Green World Championship and captain of the England team.

'Pop' was primarily a woodcutter who supplemented his income in summer by harvesting and hop picking. In his fascinating booklet The Life and Times of George Maynard, *Ken Stubbs quotes 'Pop' in an interview about hop picking:*

In the Summer I used to go out barkatching, harvesting and all such as that … hop picking, pulling the poles. I went ever so many years to the same place where I found my wife, but I went to Marden, Mr John Day's, went to him fifty-two years right off … They took me when I were a little baby, and I never missed a year, for years and years.

Pop regarded hop picking as a 'holiday with pay', with opportunities for socialising and singing in the evenings and on Sunday. He mixed with countryfolk, Londoners, Gypsies and Irish labourers and learnt many new songs, including 'The Irish Hop-Pole Puller', with its local knowledge of Kent places and pubs. Dick Richardson learnt the song from 'Pop' and suggests that the ostrich feather fashion indicates a late-Victorian or Edwardian origin, as does the reference to 'model laundries'.

George and Ron Spicer, well-known father and son singers and agricultural workers whose successive public singing careers span most of the second half of the century, both had that song in their repertoire. George came from Little Chart near Ashford. Geoff Doel (one of the authors of this book) learnt all the verses bar one from Dick Richardson and was delighted to receive a phone call from Ken Stubbs, who sang him the missing verse as he picked up the phone!

Hop-pole pulling was regarded as men's work and was higher paid than picking. The hop-pole puller used a special implement called a hop-dog to cut the bines at the base before prising up the pole with the bines still clinging to it and setting it across the hop bin ready for stripping.

I'm Coster Joe from down our street and me heart is nearly broke
I've lost me bloomin dona [girl], me coster cart and moke [donkey].
I'll tell you how it all occurred from the time we left the road
Till we got to the lovely fields of Kent.

Chorus
For she was a Model laundry girl was blue-eyed Mary Fuller
Till she went and sloped from Kent with an Irish Hop-Pole Puller.

We'd started out from the Rose and Crown with mirth and pleasure bent
We caused a big sensation in every place we went,
For Mary Ann was well dressed up in a red-plaid shawl and hat,
And a lovely ostrich feather was bought by me the flat.

We started out for Crockham Hill and then for Hunton Bull
Oh Mary Ann expressly wished for to see 'em pick and pull
I loved her so I couldn't say no and we drove down to the fields
When suddenly the cart collapsed and off came both the wheels.

My Mary called, some fellows came, I could have done without 'em,
Especially two young Irish chaps with winning ways about 'em.
One said his name was Tim and the other Mick O'Brien,
Whom I could see with half an eye my Mary fixed her eye on.

Now I flew in a jealous rage and picked a row with Tim.
Mick O' Brien he picked it up and he knocked me in the bin.
And when at last the police came and hauled me off to jail,
It's wonder I'm alive here for to tell to you the tale.

And when I came out from doing time, I found myself forsook,
For Mary Ann and Mick O'Brien had slung their bloody hook,
So if you take your dona out don't take her down to Kent,
For you'll end up broke and you'll lose your moke and you'll wish you hadn't went.

Chapter Five

The Twentieth-century Hop

Jack London (1876–1916)

'Hops and Hoppers' from *The People of the Abyss* (1903)

Jack London was born in 1876 in San Francisco. His childhood was poverty-stricken and as a youth he worked at a number of low-grade, poorly paid jobs, which caused him to write later that he had seen 'the pit, the abyss, the human cess-pool'.

As a young man in his 20s, he visited England and lived for a while in East End slums, and joined the Londoners when they went into Kent for the hop picking. The extract 'Hops and Hoppers' was written from these experiences and shows the exploitation and abuse of the poor and needy.

❧

From 'Hops and Hoppers':

So far has the divorcement of the worker from the soil proceeded, that the farming districts, the civilized world over, are dependent upon the cities for the gathering of the harvests. Then it is, when the land is spilling its ripe wealth to waste, that the street folk, who have been driven away from the soil, are called back to it again. But in England they return, not as prodigals, but as outcasts still, as vagrants and pariahs, to be doubted and flouted by their country brethren, to sleep in gaols and casual wards, or under the hedges, and to live the Lord knows how.

The hop gardens in 1867 –'Pickers Shifting Ground'. (*London Illustrated News*)

It is estimated that Kent alone requires eighty thousand of the street people to pick her hops. And out they come, obedient to the call, which is the call of their bellies and of the lingering dregs of adventure-lust still in them. Slum, stews and ghetto pour them forth, and the festering content of slum, stew and ghetto are undiminished. Yet they overrun the country like an army of ghouls, and the country does not want them. They are out of place. As they drag their squat, misshapen bodies along the highways and byways, they resemble some vile spawn from the underground. Their very presence, the fact of their existence, is an outrage to the fresh, bright sun and the green and growing things. The clean, upstanding trees cry shame upon them and their withered crookedness, and their rottenness is a slimy desecration of the sweetness and purity of nature.

Is the picture overdrawn? It all depends. For one who sees and thinks life in terms of shares and coupons, it is certainly overdrawn. But for one who sees and thinks life in terms of manhood and womanhood, it cannot be overdrawn. Such hordes of beastly wretchedness and inarticulate misery are no compensation for a millionaire brewer who lives in a West End palace, sates himself with the sensuous delights of London's golden theatres, hobnobs with lordlings and princelings, and is knighted by the King. Wins his spurs – God forbid! In old time the great blond beasts rode

83

in the battle's van and won their spurs by cleaving men from pate to chine. And, after all, it is finer to kill a strong man with a clean-slicing blow of singing steel than to make a beast of him, and of his seed through the generations, by the artful and spidery manipulation of industry and politics.

But to return to the hops. Here the divorcement from the soil is as apparent as in every other agricultural line in England. While the manufacture of beer steadily increases, the growth of hops steadily decreases. In 1835 the acreage under hops 71,327. Today it stands at 48,024, a decrease of 3,103 from the acreage of last year.

Small as the acreage is this year, a poor summer and terrible storms reduced the yield. This misfortune is divided between the people who own hops and the people who pick hops. The owners perforce must put up with less of the nicer things of life, the pickers with less grub, of which, in the best of times, they never get enough. For weary weeks headlines like the following have appeared in the London papers:

TRAMPS PLENTIFUL, BUT THE HOPS ARE FEW AND NOT YET READY

Then there have been numberless paragraphs like this:

From the neighbourhood of the hop field comes news of a distressing nature. The bright outburst of the last two days has sent many hundreds of hoppers into Kent, who will have to wait till the fields are ready for them. At Dover the number of vagrants in the workhouse is treble the number there last year at this time, and in other towns the lateness of the season is responsible for a large increase in the number of casuals.

To cap their wretchedness, when at last the picking had begun, hops and hoppers were well-nigh swept away by a frightful storm of wind, rain, and hail. The hops were stripped clean from the poles and pounded into the earth, while the hoppers, seeking shelter from the stinging hail, were close to drowning in their huts and camps on the low-lying ground. Their condition after the storm was pitiable, their state of vagrancy more pronounced than ever; for, poor crop that it was, its destruction had taken away the chance of earning a few pennies, and nothing remained for thousands of them but to 'pad the hoof' back to London.

'We ayn't crossin' sweepers,' they said, turning away from the ground, carpeted ankle-deep with hops.

Those that remained grumbled savagely among the half-stripped poles at the seven bushels for a shilling – a rate paid in good seasons when the hops are in prime condition, and a rate likewise paid in bad seasons by the growers because they cannot afford more.

I passed through Teston and East and West Farleigh shortly after the storm and listened to the grumbling of the hoppers and saw the hops rotting on the ground. At the hothouses of Barham Court, thirty thousand panes of glass had been broken by the hail, while peaches, plums, pears, apples, rhubarb, cabbages, mangolds, everything had been pounded to pieces and torn to shreds.

All of which was too bad for the owners, certainly; but at the worst, not one of them, for one meal, would have to go short of food or drink. Yet it was to them that the newspapers devoted columns of sympathy, their pecuniary losses being detailed at harrowing length. 'Mr Herbert L– calculates his loss at £8,000'; 'Mr F–, of brewery fame, who rents all the land in this parish, loses £10,000'; and 'Mr L–, the Wateringbury brewer, brother to Mr Herbert L–, is another heavy loser.' As for the hoppers, they did not count. Yet I venture to assert that the several almost-square meals lost by the underfed William Buggles, and underfed Mrs Buggles, and the underfed Buggles kiddies, was a greater tragedy than the £10,000 lost by Mr F–. And, in addition, underfed William Buggles' tragedy might be multiplied by thousands where Mr F– 's could not be multiplied by five.

To see how William Buggles and his kind fared, I donned my seafaring togs and started out to get a job. With me was a young East London cobbler, Bert, who had yielded to the lure of adventure and joined me for the trip. Acting on my advice, he had brought his 'worst rags', and as we hiked up the London road out of Maidstone he was worrying greatly for fear we had come too ill-dressed for the business.

Nor was he to be blamed. When we stopped in a tavern the publican eyed us gingerly, nor did his demeanour brighten till we showed him the colour of our cash. The natives along the coast were all dubious; and 'beanfeasters' from London, dashing past in coaches, cheered and jeered and shouted insulting things after us. But before we were done with the Maidstone district my friend found that we were as well clad, if not better, than the average hopper. Some of the bunches of rags we chanced upon were marvellous.

'The tide is out,' called a Gypsy-looking woman to her mates as we came up a long row of bins into which the pickers were stripping the hops.

'Do you twig?' Bert whispered. 'She's on to you.'

I twigged. And it must be confessed the figure was an apt one. When the tide is out boats are left on the beach and do not sail, and a sailor, when the tide is out, does not sail either. My seafaring togs and my presence in the hop field proclaimed that I was a seaman without a ship, a man on the beach, and very like a craft at low water.

'Can yer give us a job, governor?' Bert asked the bailiff, a kindly faced and elderly man who was very busy.

His 'No' was decisively uttered; but Bert clung on and followed him about, and I followed after, pretty well all over the field. Whether our persistency struck the bailiff as anxiety to work, or whether he was affected by our hard-luck appearance and tale, neither Bert nor I succeeded in making out; but in the end he softened his heart and found us the one unoccupied bin in the place – a bin deserted by two other men, from what I could learn, because of inability to make living wages.

'No bad conduct, mind ye,' warned the bailiff, as he left us at work in the midst of the women.

It was Saturday afternoon, and we knew quitting time would come early; so we applied ourselves earnestly to the task, desiring to learn if we could at least make our salt. It was simple work, woman's work, in fact, and not man's. We sat on the edge of the bin, between the standing hops, while a pole-puller supplied us with great fragrant branches. In an hour's time we became as expert as it is possible to become. As soon as the fingers became accustomed automatically to differentiate between hops and leaves and to strip half-a-dozen blossoms at a time there was no more to learn.

We worked nimbly, and as fast as the women themselves, though their bins filled more rapidly because of their swarming children, each of which picked with two hands almost as fast as we picked.

'Don'tcher pick too clean it's against the rules,' one of the women informed us; and we took the tip and were grateful.

As the afternoon wore along, we realized that living wages could not be made – by men. Women could pick as much as men, and children could do almost as well as women; so it was impossible for a man to compete with a woman and half-a-dozen children who could count as a unit, and by their combined capacity determine the unit's pay.

'I say, matey, I'm beastly hungry,' said I to Bert. We had not had any dinner.

'Blimey, but I could eat the 'ops,' he replied.

Whereupon we both lamented our negligence in not rearing up a numerous progeny to help us in this day of need. And in such fashion we whiled away the time and talked for the edification of our neighbours. We quite won the sympathy of the pole-puller, a young country yokel, who now and again, emptied a few picked blossoms into our bin, it being part of his business to gather up the stray clusters torn off in the process of pulling.

With him we discussed how much we could 'sub', and were informed that while we were being paid a shilling for seven bushels, we could only 'sub', or have advanced to us, a shilling for every twelve bushels. Which is to say that the pay for five out of every twelve bushels was withheld – a method of the growers to hold the hopper to his work whether the crop runs good or bad, and especially if it runs bad.

After all, it was pleasant sitting there in the bright sunshine, the golden pollen showering from our hands, the pungent aromatic odour of the hops biting our nostrils, and the while remembering dimly the sounding cities whence these people came. Poor street people! Poor gutter folk! Even they grow earth-hungry, and yearn vaguely for the soil from which they have been driven, and for the free life in the open, and the wind and rain and sun all undefiled by city smirches. As the sea calls to the sailor, so calls the land to them; and, deep down in their aborted and decaying carcasses, they are stirred strangely by the peasant memories of their forebears who lived before cities were. And in incomprehensible ways they are made glad by the earth smells and sights and sounds which their blood has not forgotten though unremembered by them.

'No more 'ops, matey,' Bert complained.

It was five o'clock, and the pole-pullers had knocked off, so that everything could be cleaned up, there being no work on Sunday. For an hour we were forced idly to wait the coming of the measurers, our feet tingling with the frost which came on the heels of the setting sun. In the adjoining bin, two women and half-a-dozen children had picked nine bushels: so that the five bushels the measurers found in our bin demonstrated that we had done equally well, for the half-dozen children had ranged from nine to fourteen years of age.

Five bushels! We worked it out to eightpence ha'penny, or seventeen cents, for two men working three hours and a half. Fourpence farthing apiece! A little over a penny an hour! But we were allowed only to 'sub' fivepence of the total sum, though the tallykeeper, short of change, gave us sixpence. Entreaty was in vain. A hard-luck story could not move him. He proclaimed loudly that we had received a penny more than our due, and went his way.

Granting, for the sake of the argument, that we were what we represented ourselves to be –namely, poor men and broke – then here was our position: night was coming on; we had had no supper, much less dinner; and we possessed sixpence between us. I was hungry enough to eat three sixpenn'orths of food, and so was Bert. One thing was patent. By doing sixteen and one third per cent justice to our stomachs, we would expend the sixpence, and our stomachs would still be gnawing under eighty three and two thirds per cent injustice. Being broke again, we could sleep under a hedge, which was not so bad, though the cold would sap an undue portion of what we had eaten. But the morrow was Sunday, on which we could do no work, though our silly stomachs would not knock off on that account. Here, then was the problem: how to get three meals on Sunday, and two on Monday (for we could not make another 'sub' till Monday evening). We knew that the casual wards were overcrowded; also, that if we begged from farmer or villager, there was a large likelihood of our going to gaol for fourteen days. What was to be done? We looked at each other in despair –

Not a bit of it. We joyfully thanked God that we were not as other men, especially hoppers, and went down the road to Maidstone, jingling in our pockets the half-crowns and florins we had brought from London.

Rudyard Kipling (1865–1936)

'Dymchurch Flit' from *Puck of Pook's Hill* (1906)

Rudyard Kipling leapt into fame when he was just 20 years old, earning his living as a journalist in India and writing in his spare time. By the 1890s his name was a household word in England and America and in 1907 he was awarded the ultimate accolade – the Nobel Prize for Literature.

In 1899 he and his family settled in 'Bateman's', an imposing seventeenth-century house outside the village of Burwash in Sussex. Kipling lived here for thirty-four years and Puck of Pook's Hill *was directly inspired by his children's fanciful name for a hilly rise in the grounds. The book is a collection of stories of England through the ages and in 'Dymchurch Flit' the goblin Puck summons up spirits from the past before two Edwardian children, Una and Dan, inspired by Kipling's own children. The scene opens in a hop yard, and then moves into the oast house where the hops are being turned continuously in order to ensure even drying. Una and Dan, as was the common practice of children involved in hopping, have taken potatoes to be roasted in the ashes. The drier is no ordinary mortal – he is revealed to be the sprite Puck.*

✤✤✤

From 'Dymchurch Flit':

Just at dusk, a soft September rain began to fall on the hop-pickers. The mothers wheeled the bouncing perambulators out of the gardens; bins were put away, and tally-books made up. The young couples strolled home, two to each umbrella, and the single men walked behind them laughing. Dan and Una, who had been picking after their lessons, marched off to roast potatoes at the oast-house, where old Hobden, with Blue-eyed Bess, his lurcher dog, lived all the month through, drying the hops.

They settled themselves, as usual, on the sack-strewn cot in front of the fires, and, when Hobden drew up the shutter, stared, as usual, at the flameless bed of coals spouting its heat up the dark well of the old-fashioned roundel. Slowly he

Rudyard Kipling. (Library of Congress LC-USZ62-118996)

cracked off a few fresh pieces of coal, packed them, with fingers that never flinched, exactly where they would do most good; slowly he reached behind him till Dan tilted the potatoes into his iron scoop of a hand; carefully he arranged them round the fire, and then stood for a moment, black against the glare. As he closed the shutter, the oast-house seemed dark before the day's end, and he lit the candle in the lanthorn. The children liked all these things because they knew them so well.

The Bee Boy, Hobden's son, who is not quite right in his head, though he can do anything with bees, slipped in like a shadow. They only guessed it when Bess's stump-tail wagged against them.

A big voice began singing outside in the drizzle:

'Old Mother Laidinwool had nigh twelve months been dead,
She heard the hops were doin' well, and then popped up her head.'

'There can't be two people made to holler like that!' cried old Hobden, wheeling round.

'"For," says she, "The boys I've picked with when I was young and fair,
They're bound to be at hoppin', and I'm– "'

A man showed at the doorway.
'Well, well! They do say hoppin'll draw the very deadest, and now I belieft 'em. You, Tom? Tom Shoesmith?' Hobden lowered his lanthorn.

'You're a hem of a time makin' your mind to it, Ralph!' The stranger strode in – three full inches taller than Hobden, a grey-whiskered, brown-faced giant with clear blue eyes. They shook hands, and the children could hear the hard palms rasp together.

'You ain't lost none o' your grip,' says Hobden. 'Was it thirty or forty year back you broke my head at Peasmarsh Fair?'

'Only thirty, an' no odds 'tween us regardin' heads, neither. You had it back at me with a hop-pole. How did we get home that night? Swimmin'?'

'Same way the pheasant come into Gubbs's pocket – by a little luck an' a deal o' conjurin'.' Old Hobden laughed in his deep chest.

'I see you've not forgot your way about the woods. D'ye do any o' *this* still?' The stranger pretended to look along a gun.

Hobden answered with a quick movement of the hand as though he were pegging down a rabbit-wire.

'No. *That's* all that's left me now. Age she must as Age she can. An' what's your news since all these years?'

'Oh, I've bin to Plymouth, I've bin to Dover –
I've bin ramblin', boys, the wide world over,'

The man answered cheerily. 'I reckon I know as much of Old England as most.'
He turned towards the children and winked boldly.

'I lay they told you a sight o' lies, then. I've been into England fur as Wiltsheer
once. I was cheated proper over a pair of hedgin'-gloves,' said Hobden.

'There's fancy-talkin' everywhere. *You've* cleaved to your own parts pretty
middlin' close, Ralph.'

'Can't shift an old tree 'thout it dyin',' Hobden chuckled. 'An' I be no more
anxious to die than you look to be to help me with my hops to-night.'

The great man leaned against the brickwork of the roundel, and swung his
arms abroad. 'Hire me!' was all he said, and they stumped upstairs laughing.

The children heard their shovels rasp on the cloth where the yellow hops lie
drying above the fires, and all the oast-house filled with the sweet, sleepy smell as
they were turned.

'Who is it?' Una whispered to the Bee Boy.

'Dunno, no more'n you – if *you* dunno,' said he, and smiled.

The voices on the drying-floor talked together, and the heavy footsteps
moved back and forth. Presently a hop-pocket dropped through the press-hole
over-head, and stiffened and fattened as they shovelled it full. 'Clank!' went the
press and rammed the loose stuff into tight cake.

'Gentle!' they heard Hobden cry. 'You'll bust her crop if you lay on so. You be
as careless as Gleason's bull, Tom. Come an' sit by the fires. She'll do now.'

They came down, and as Hobden opened the shutter to see if the potatoes
were done, Tom Shoesmith said to the children, 'Put a plenty salt on 'em. That'll
show you the sort o' man *I* be.' Again he winked, and again the Bee Boy laughed
and Una stared at Dan.

'*I* know what sort o' man you be,' old Hobden grunted, groping for the
potatoes round the fire.

❧❧❧

In the sequel, Rewards and Fairies, *there is an interesting hop-picking metaphor:*

The Boy's fine green-and-gold clothes were torn all to pieces, and he had been
welted by the woman's nails to pieces. He looked like a Robertsbridge hopper on
a Monday morning.

Edmund Blunden (1896–1974)

'The Midnight Skaters' from the Collection
Poems of Many Years (1957)

Blunden in his poetry often evokes the great beauty of the Kent countryside, and couples it with a sense of melancholy or malaise. 'The Midnight Skater' is typical of his work in this respect. He sets the scene in a hop-garden in winter. It appears to be a scene of great beauty – the hop-poles, grouped in cones, stand motionless in white fields under a darkened sky while youths and children skate joyously on a frozen pond. For Blunden, death lurks in the fathomless deeps but the young people are lost in their pleasures and oblivious to all danger.

Blunden's acute sense of impending death derived from his wartime experiences as a young soldier in the First World War.

The Midnight Skaters

The hop-poles stand in cones,
The icy pond lurks under,
The pole-tops steeple to the thrones
Of stars, sound gulfs of wonder;
But not the tallest there, 'tis said,
Could fathom to this pond's black bed.

Then is not death at watch
Within those secret waters?
What wants he but to catch
Earth's heedless sons and daughters?
With but a crystal parapet
Between, he has his engines set.

Then on, blood shouts, on, on,
'Twirl, wheel and whip above him,
Dance on this ball-floor thin and wan,
Use him as though you love him
Court him, elude him, reel and pass,
And let him hate you through the glass.

Sheila Kaye-Smith (1887–1956)

'The Shepherd of Lattenden' from *Sussex Saints* (1926)

Sheila Kaye-Smith is accounted Sussex's only regional novelist. She was intensely religious and imbued the Sussex landscape with mysticism in her novels, plays and poems. She and her husband bought and restored an isolated oast house to live in at Little Doucegrove between Northiam and Brede and in 1956 she fell to her death down the spiral staircase which led to her study, in a converted oast kiln.

    Sussex Saints consists of a series of poems and plays which retell aspects of the Christian story, using rural Sussex settings, occupations and speech patterns. 'The Shepherd of Lattenden' is a Passion play set in the environs of Rye, and scene two sets the betrayal of Christ (the Shepherd of Lattenden) in the hop garden at Doleham, instead of Gethsemane.

❧❧❧

From 'The Shepherd of Lattenden':

Scene 2:

Scene: *The Hop Garden at Doleham. The Easter moon is bright. She is like a ship sailing the dark waters of the sky. Though she rides smoothly there is about her an air of terror, as if once more the waters of space were in storm. Her radiance has wiped out the stars. It sweeps down into the hop-garden of Doleham, bathing it in a flood of light so brilliant that colours are visible – the green of the hedge, with the yellow clumps of the primroses beneath it, the green of the young bines, only half-way to their crowns. Over the hedge rise the oast-houses of Doleham, their roofs shining red in the celestial light. A distant song is heard. It draws nearer, and the words of a psalm are distinguishable.*

Voices	Hear me, O Lord, for thy loving-kindness is comfortable: turn thee unto me according to the multitude of thy mercies. And hide not thy face from thy servant, for I am in trouble: O haste thee and hear me. Draw nigh unto my soul and save it: O deliver me because of mine enemies.

(*The Shepherd enters the hop-garden with Peter, James and John, singing as they walk. They look tired and beaten.*)

Disciples (singing)   Thou hast known my reproof, my shame and my
dishonour: mine adversaries are all in thy sight.
Thy rebuke hath broken my heart; I am full of heaviness:
I looked for some to have pity on me, but there was no
man, neither found I any to comfort me.

Peter (breaking up the singing and throwing himself upon the ground)
Reckon I'm tired.

James and John (also throwing themselves down)
And I –

(The Shepherd remains standing before them)

Shepherd   I am full of heaviness.

Peter   So are we all. Master, sit down and rest.
Reckon we've come further than we should ought.

(The Shepherd shakes his head.)

Shepherd   My soul is sorrowful. I am afraid.
Wait here with me while I pray. Do not leave me.

Peter (lazily)   We aren't likely to run away, Shepherd. We're too mortal tired.

*(The Shepherd looks at them sadly, then goes off among the hop-bines which have made
him a tent of shadow. The three disciples settle themselves under the hedge. The voices of
hidden and grieving angels are heard. Their singing is like the sigh of the wind through
the hedge and through the hop-bines – there are tears in it like hidden water. It is sweet,
and not quite human, for the angels do not grieve as man, their grief belongs to the ages
before the world began, and is like the voice of stars singing sorrowfully together.)*

Angel Choir
V   In the hop-garden he prayed, saying
O my Father, if it be possible let this cup pass from me.
The Spirit indeed is willing
But the flesh is weak.

B	Watch and pray That ye enter not into temptation. The spirit indeed is willing But the flesh is weak.
John	Did you hear that? Was that music?
Peter	I don't like it. I'm afraid here.

(They huddle closer to one another.)

James	I don't like any of it – anything that's happening now. It's all changed, somehow. We were doing valiant, and now– I don't know what it is, but it's different.
Peter	Let's have a bit of sleep.
John	He asked us to keep watch.
James	He's gone away. He's forgotten all about us.
Peter	He can't expect us to keep awake all night.
John	We might put up a bit of a prayer.
James	You can if you like. I'm too sleepy. Look – Peter's off.

(Peter's head has fallen on John's shoulder. James drops his upon the other. For a moment John sits manfully with head erect, eyes gazing into the darkness under the hop-bines, then his head too falls on his breast. There is silence for a while. – Then the voice of the Shepherd is heard in the distance raised sharply and suddenly in great agony.)

Shepherd (off)	Father, if it be possible let this cup pass from me. Nevertheless not my will but thine be done.

(There is another silence, more terrible than any music. But the companions are not afraid. They are asleep. The voice of the ANGELS *comes again like the voice of the moonlight.)*

Angel Choir

V   My soul is exceeding sorrowful, even unto death
                  Tarry ye here and watch with me.
                  Even now shall ye see the multitude
                  Which shall come about me.
                  Ye shall flee, and I go to be offered up for you.

B   Behold the hour is at hand,
                  And the Son of Man is betrayed to sinners.
                  Ye shall flee, and I go to be offered up for you.

(The silence broods for an instant, then is rent again as with a sword. The voice of the Shepherd comes from the darkness.)

Shepherd   Father, if this cup may not pass from me except
                  I drink it – thy will be done.

(The Shepherd comes out into the moonlight. He looks round for his companions, then sees them sleeping under the hedge. He stands gazing down at them, while the invisible ANGELS *sing, answering each other thus.)*

Angel Choir

V   What! Could ye not watch with me one hour
                  Who were ready to die for me?
                  Or see ye not Judas. How he sleepeth not,
                  But hasteneth to betray me?

B   Why sleep ye? Watch and pray
                  That ye enter not into temptation.
                  Or see ye not Judas, how he sleepeth not,
                  But hasteneth to betray me?

(The Shepherd stoops as if to wake the three disciples, but suddenly there is a muffled sound of footsteps and voices beyond the hedge. He straightens himself and looks swiftly up to the moon. As the sounds draw nearer the companions begin to wake, stretching themselves, and yawning.)

Peter   What's that?

James   There's someone on the road.

John *(springing to his feet)*
                          He has come back, our Shepherd, and found us sleeping.

Shepherd   It is enough. The hour is come.
                          (He stands motionless by the little knot of his disciples.)

Peter *(terrified)*   They're after us. They've tracked us down.

James *(looking through the hedge)*
                          It's that scum Judas.

John   Oh Master, Master, whatsumever shall we do?

James   Let's get off quickly.

(At that moment Judas comes creeping through the hedge.
He runs to the Shepherd and kisses him shamefacedly.)

Judas   Master, Master!

Shepherd   Why have you come friend?

Judas   Master, I want a word with you.

James   Don't trust him – he's up to no good.
                          Come, let's get off while there's time.

(At that a dozen of the rural constabulary break through the hedge, carrying torches
and lanterns. Their truncheons are drawn and they advance towards the Shepherd,
who stands motionless.)

Shepherd   Are you coming to take a thief?

Judas *(his embrace changing to a grip)*
                          Here he is. Hold him fast.

(For some reason the constabulary do not come any further. They stand in a little huddle by the hedge. Judas suddenly drops his arms and shrinks back among them.)

Shepherd   What have you come for?

A Voice   The Shepherd of Lattenden.

Shepherd   Here I am.

(Still nobody moves. The Shepherd stands for a calm instant. Then challenges again.)

Shepherd   What do you want?

A Voice   The Shepherd of Lattenden.

Shepherd   I've told you who I am. But if you want me, let these go.
        (Pointing to the three disciples.)

(Without waiting for the answer, the companions turn suddenly and disappear into the darkness of the hop-bines.)

Shepherd   Shall I not drink the cup which my Father has given me?

(The little band of captors now suddenly seems to recover its senses. It closes round the Shepherd, seizes him, and huddles him off through the torn hedge. The hop-garden is empty. The ship of the moon still sails the Easter midnight. The voices of the ANGELS creep through the silence.)

Angel Choir
V   I was like a lamb that is innocent:
        I was brought to the slaughter, and I knew it not:
        Mine enemies have taken counsel against me,
        Saying:
        Come, let us put wood in his bread,
        Let us root him out
        From the land of the living.

B
All mine enemies have taken counsel
And have spoken unjustly against me,
Saying:
Come, let us put wood in his bread,
Let us root him out
From the land of the Living.

Rules to Pickers from the Beltring Whitbread Hop Farm (1930s)

This substantial farm is now an excellent museum. The oast farm demanded good behaviour from their pickers but rewarded the workers well with a Harvest Supper at the end of the picking as did many other hop farms locally. Sometimes the supper was set out in the oast house where the hops were dried. In the early days elected 'Kings' and 'Queens of the Hop' were garlanded with hops and 'presided' over the party. Other farms, possibly influenced by the Temperance Movement, preferred to give a tea party for the children. At Beltring, Whitbread's hop farm, there was a Hop-Queen competition, entered by the prettiest girls from each of the hop-gardens. After her 'crowning', the elected 'Whitbread Queen' was dressed in a velvet cloak and given a bouquet of hops, after which she was drawn round the farm in a hop cart pulled by two carthorses.

Rules to Pickers

1.- Bin-Tickets are supplied on the understanding that holders guarantee sufficient picking strength at the bins. Each Bin-Ticket should represent at least two adults, with family under 14 years of age, and ticket-holders who fail to supply this picking strength will not be granted tickets in future.

2.- Pickers who, after receiving tickets, find that they are unable to get away, must either return the tickets promptly to us, or be responsible for the good behaviour of the persons to whom they give the tickets.

3.- Pickers will be notified in good time when to come down for the picking. Persons arriving before such notice is received by them will be refused admission.

4.- Bookers have special instructions to collect all tickets before pickers commence work. Persons unable to produce official tickets will be refused.

5.- Watchmen are employed solely for the purpose of attending to pickers' wants as to straw, firing, etc., and any complaint must be made to them. Pickers who cannot get reasonable attention should mention the matter at the Farm Office.

6.- Firing is put down at each house or tent every day. Any person taking firing belonging to someone else, or otherwise committing wanton mischief, will be immediately discharged and paid off at the rate of one penny per basket for hops picked.

7.- After the tally has been set, and not dissented from, anyone going on strike, or leaving work during a strike, or leaving the picking before it is finished, will be paid off at one penny per basket.

8.- Anyone damaging fruit trees will be at once discharged.

9.- Pickers are warned to be very careful with all lights as a precaution against fire. It must be clearly understood that all goods brought down by pickers are held by them entirely at their own risk, and the Company does not accept any liability for any damage or loss to Hop-Pickers' effects while on the Farm.

10.- Pickers who desire bin-tickets, but have not held them before, should write stating the number of the Company in which they worked the previous year.

11.- When application is made for tickets it is important that changes of name and address should be clearly notified.

12.- Although ample hut accommodation is provided, pickers are requested to assist us in preventing over-crowding, by only bringing down their *own* children.

13.- Dogs are not permitted on the Farm, and watchmen have instructions to refuse pickers who bring them.

14.- Pickers are expected to put all refuse into the dustbins provided, and occupiers of huts will be held responsible for the proper use and condition of the dustbins allotted to them.

15.- No person (adult or child) who, at any time during the 14 days prior to the commencement of picking, has been in contact with a person suffering from any infectious or contagious disease will be allowed on the Farm. This rule will be strictly enforced, and ticket-holders will be responsible for the pickers who accompany them.

Every letter is answered whenever possible by return of post. Any applicant therefore not receiving a reply within four days should write again, being very careful to give the proper address.

As in the past, we desire to make the pickers as comfortable as possible, and their assistance is looked for to aid us in this.

FINALLY the hops must be picked cleanly, and not in bunches. Any picker disregarding this rule will be discharged, and not allowed to come another year.

WHITBREAD & CO. LTD
J.H. Waghorn,
FARM MANAGER

George Orwell (1903–1950)

From 'Hop Picking' (1931)

George Orwell kept a notebook in 1931, which he later remodelled as an essay entitled 'Hop Picking', in which he recorded his eighteen days' experience as a picker in a hop garden at Wateringbury in the Medway Valley near Maidstone. Orwell's companion was an experienced tramp and ex-convict called Ginger and they supplemented their rations by stealing and begging. Having no money they slept rough or in workhouse dormitories en route to the farms and when employed Orwell records they were housed by the hop farmers either in disused stables, which Orwell found dry and relatively warm, or in round tin hoppers' huts, which were cold and uncomfortable and overfull. Orwell's fellow pickers were costers from the East End of London, poor Irish, Gypsies and 'gentlemen of the road'. The evenings were spent frying up supper on a tin lid and stealing from the surrounding fruit farms. On Sundays they washed their shirts and socks in the stream and slept. Orwell concludes that the work was virtually slave labour, but enjoyed the Saturday

Hop-growers' strike, Tonbridge, 1908 – joined by the hop-pickers. (Fran & Geoff Doel Collection)

nights when camp fires were lit and apples were roasted in the flames and the majority of the men got drunk.

Orwell used these experiences as the basis for his autobiographical work Down and Out in Paris and London *(1933) and a novel,* A Clergyman's Daughter *(1935).*

❧❧❧

From 'Hop Picking' (1931):

One can't earn 30s a week or anything near it. It is a curious fact, though, that very few of the pickers were aware how little they really earned, because the piece-work system disguises the low rate of payment.

When one starts work the farm gives one a printed copy of rules, which are designed to reduce a picker more or less to a slave. According to these rules the farmer can sack a picker without notice and on any pretext whatever, and pay him off at eight bushels a shilling instead of six – i.e. confiscate a quarter of his earnings. If a picker leaves his job before the picking is finished his earnings are docked the same amount. You cannot draw what you have earned and then clear off, because the farm will never pay you more than two thirds of your earnings in advance, and so are in your debt till the last day. The bin-men (i.e. foreman) get wages instead of being paid on the piece-work system, and these wages cease if there is a strike, so naturally they will raise heaven and earth to prevent one. Altogether the farmers have the hop-pickers in a cleft stick, and always will have until there is a pickers' union. It is not much use to try and form a union, though, for about half the pickers are women and gypsies, and are too stupid to see the advantages of it.

Miles Sargent

'The Day's Work' from *St Francis of the Hop-Fields* (1933)

All kinds of philanthropic Christian bodies in the nineteenth and twentieth centuries took an interest in the physical, spiritual and moral welfare of the hoppers. One of the most famous workers in the field was an Anglican priest from St Augustine's, Stepney. His name was Father Richard Wilson. So many of his parishioners in the East End left the city in the hop-picking season and disappeared into Kent that in 1898 he decided to join them in the hop-gardens. One particular image haunted him – that of a young mother who had walked five miles carrying her dead baby in a brown paper bag. The following year, Father Wilson took action. He rented a cottage on the green at Five Oaks Green and opened it to the hoppers as a kind of medical centre. This became the first of three buildings which were to be known as the 'Little Hoppers Hospital'. Here he worked with three volunteer nurses and they attended to the sick amongst the pickers. Their work was inspirational. It inspired other missions, this time from three universities, Cambridge, Oxford, and London. Christian undergraduates, trainee priests and private individuals linked with the universities all came to the hop-fields and worked as volunteers among the hop pickers.

The third building used as a hospital was of sixteenth-century origin and formerly used as a pub; it is still known as 'The Hoppers Hospital' and still has links with the church in Stepney, being used as a religious retreat and often open to the public on Heritage Days.

Twenty-seven years after opening his first 'hospital', in 1925 Father Wilson and Miles Sargent started a new centre at Crowhurst, this time staffed by Oxford undergraduates and medical students. Other 'missions' followed – but the object was always to give the hop pickers free medical advice, to hold religious services on Sunday mornings and to provide a Sunday school for the children. The last was always very well attended. Though the adult hoppers seemed impervious to Christianity, they adored Father Wilson and his nurses and young medical students. The universities'

Sign for the Hoppers Hospital. (Fran & Geoff Doel Collection)

young teams in the hospital and gardens were treated with warmth and affection and particularly appreciated for the tea-barrow which they pushed through the hop gardens every day and became something of a legend.

The Missions ended before the final phase of hop picking.

The extracts from Miles Sargent's lively and informative 1933 article below describe the tea-barrow, the dramatic putting out of a fire, and the Saturday-night drinking.

⁂⁂

Extracts from *St Francis of the Hop-Fields*:

'The barrow' is a vehicle which holds a large tank which is filled with tea. It is then dragged or pushed up amongst the pickers who have been at work since seven-thirty, and large mugs of tea are sold at a halfpenny each. Cakes and buns are sold at the same time and provide a 'levener' which is very welcome.

The water for the barrow is boiled up in a large boiler … known as 'The Rocket'. As we only burn wood, it needs a lot of attention … A tremendous amount of tradition has grown up around the travels of the barrow. It needs a team of at least four to work it properly, and the team has also to act as a male choir, since everything 'down picking is done with a song, and a dance too if possible'. Its entry to the hop-lines is announced by the singing of two lines of a Yiddish song:

Yoi, yoi, what a gime it is
What a gime it is
Yoi, yoi!

This is sung to a very good plainsong melody, not of our invention; we took it over with the song. Then comes an hour or more of chaffering and back-chat. Jokes are cracked and personalities bandied to and fro, until the tanks run dry and the cakes are sold and the barrow bumps it way back to the Mission, to rest for another twenty-two hours. The surgery opens at half-past nine for an hour, and special cases are then attended to.

… just as we had finished tea, we saw clouds of smoke pouring from a hut which was in the middle of a long row. Off we all dashed, to find a dense crowd of pickers standing round helpless and inactive. We went straight through them and got to the door of the hut, which was half open. Someone screamed that there were children inside. I went in first and took a look around, but it was impossible to stay in more than a second or two, owing to the dense fumes of the burning straw. The flames were beginning to lick up from the bed and from the curtains, which were hung on the walls as a decoration and draught-excluder. Hugh Davies went in next, and came out almost as quickly as I did. He was as sure as I that there was no one in there. Then Tom Rice went in, and by this time some one had got a bucket of water. He upped and slung it well into the doorway, and Tom caught the lot in the back of the neck.

By this time Hugh and I had organised a chain of kettles, as fortunately every one was getting water for tea, and Joe and Tom Boase had got rakes and forks and were pulling the burning contents of the hut out into the open. Soon all was extinguished and then the owners of the hut arrived. They were old Mrs Walters, who was born in a hop house and had never missed a picking in her life, and her son, Joe Bilby, a man about forty years of age better known amongst his pals as Joby. We never solved the mystery of how that fire started, or how it was that a girl who lived next door had a pair of 'Russian boots' burnt, and where she got the idea that the Mission had to pay her compensation. She didn't get the compensation, but it was a long time before she gave up hope.

Up at the 'boozer' that night our deeds of prowess grew to enormous proportions, and these rather startling happenings were forcing in on the pickers' minds that we were there with a purpose, and that that purpose was to do what we could to help them. Next day we were asked to pick the padlock of a hut, and we managed it quite nicely.

On the Saturday night we were introduced to another phase of life on a hop-garden, a phase to which we soon got used and which is now a thing of the past as far as we can tell. It was the return from the public house. Until we started our canteen in 1931 there was no place of meeting for the pickers after the day's work was done, except the two public houses, The Fountain and The Bush. Crowds used to flock up every night because there was nowhere else to go, and at closing time they used to wend their way, devious or otherwise, back to the farm. The Londoner is *afraid of the dark* because he is not used to it. At home the streets are lighted all night, and there are friendly policemen about, and belated taxis and lorries and street cleaners, and a host of workers whom the ordinary daylight folk never see. But in the country the lanes are dark, and for all you know, the hedges may be bristling with highwaymen and robbers. So the pickers come down from the public house in large companies, singing and dancing quite good-humouredly, chiefly to keep their spirits up during the venturesome journey. Their fear of the dark is a very real fear, and I remember once a woman coming down to the Mission when night had fallen and asking for the 'lend' of a kettle-full of water. As we never lend anything, on principle, I suggested that she should go to the tap which was about a hundred and fifty yards away across the field. 'What?' she replied, 'Me go down there all that way alone in the dark? Why, I should scream all the way there and back!'

Vita Sackville-West (1892–1962)

'The Hop-Picking Season' and
'The Garden and the Oast' from *Country Notes* (1939)

Vita Sackville-West, aristocrat, writer and gardener extraordinaire, wrote numbers of essays and articles for magazines whilst restoring and living in Sissinghurst Castle and creating the famous 7-acres garden which is now owned by the National Trust. In 1939 these pieces were made into a collection and published by Michael Joseph under the title Country Notes. *As a farmer herself who owned the 200-acre Bettenham Farm, Vita was interested in hop picking as a business concern and a phenomena of Kent life. In the following resumes of these articles (though the first may seem too romanticised and slightly condescending towards the workers) both essays are actually well researched and very informative.*

In 'The Hop-Picking Season' Sackville-West considers the London hop-picking workforce that at that moment is invading her home county of Kent. She informs us from the moment that London's hop pickers leave their 'slums' in Bermondsey they cease to be ' rather vulgar' and assume a romantic aspect This is in part she thinks due to the colourful picture they present, the jaunty red kerchiefs knotted round the men's throats and the garishly coloured muslin frocks worn by their womenfolk as they pick in the gardens – for her they assume the romanticised image of the Gypsy who is regarded by the English, she implies, as something exotic and colourful. Seeing the pickers working in the gardens alongside their children reminds this well-travelled aristocrat of the Neapolitan peasant workforce labouring hard under a blazing sun, gaily harvesting the Muscat variety of grape – although she admits that the English in general are rather less 'gay' than their Italian counterparts. Vita has inquired about their sleeping arrangements and has seen inside the hoppers' huts. She describes them as being lime-washed inside

Sissinghurst Castle and gardens. (Fran & Geoff Doel Collection)

and provided with a bench and some straw. The purpose-built accommodation cannot house everyone, she tells us, and a few families make do with some old railways coaches. She informs us that the families have brought all kinds of colourful bedding and knick-knacks from home with which they personalise and decorate the interiors, turning the little 'hovels' into veritable 'Dutch paintings'. She finishes with an idealised picture of the end of their day when exhausted from their labours and with a glass of beer in their hand they contentedly gather in family groups round a blazing fire, singing lustily to tunes played on accordions in the gathering gloom.

'The Garden and the Oast' is less romanticised and deals primarily but not mundanely with the technicalities involved in hop production – the preparation of the ground, the stringing done by the women and children working round the bottom of the vine, the permanent wires fixed overhead by men on stilts, the mechanics of drying the hops in hot fumes on the floor of the oast house and the bagging of the hops into pockets after which they are carted away to the brewers. This is an accurate, concise and very readable account of hop farming containing some less well-known snippets of information that would interest a farmer, such as the fact that bines will only grow round the string from right to left and cannot be trained to do otherwise.

Vita's rather romanticised idea of Gypsies may have been inspired by her research into the extraordinary life of her own maternal grandmother, Pepita, a Spanish Gypsy and flamenco dancer, whose 'life' she had written and had published just two years before in 1937.

There is a charming end to the last of these two essays when Sackville-West, on witnessing the departure of the Londoners from the hop gardens, concludes unexpectedly and rather endearingly, 'I shall miss the Hoppers'.

Ken Thompson

Running a Hop Farm

Ken Thompson spent his early life working on his father's farm, 'Little Betsoms' on the North Downs, which he managed for a while after his father's death. Ken then tried his hand at fruit-farming in the Vale of Evesham, before managing a hop-farm in Faversham in the 1950s and 1960s during the transition from hand-picking to mechanisation. Ken's vivid reminiscences are especially interesting in demonstrating a hop-farmer's viewpoint and in recording the end of an era.

Hop Farming in the 1950s and early 1960s
(from Ken's oral recollections transcribed by Fran Doel (1990))

When I got involved with the hops in the '50s it was just becoming modernised. Some of the hops were picked by machine, some were picked by hand. You had what was called a tally – a tally of pickers is about fifty women and you had the machines working as well. We took on probably 300 or 400 hand-pickers at the beginning of the season and probably sixty to seventy casuals for working the hop-picking machines. There was a right old mixture of people when we were hopping. We had the job of organising and getting all the hop-pickers in from south-east London, the Medway towns and Dover, and all round. Some used to come by train on 'The Hoppers' Specials' and we

Ken Thompson (left) at his Faversham hop farm, 1950s. (Fran & Geoff Doel Collection)

used to fetch them from Faversham station by lorry. The station used to be one mass of hoppers with their gear and all sorts. We had no gypsies. Not on my particular farm.

We had hoppers' huts – no tents. They weren't that marvellous, the huts – wooden walls and corrugated iron roofs – but the pickers used to make them comfortable, and the fires got going outside of the huts at night. Two or three families to the huts depending on the size of the family. They used to paper them and the governor used to curse and say that all the bugs in the world got behind them.

The men and women did different jobs. Basically the men were pole-pullers. When it was hand picking the men pulled the hops down and did the measuring and the carrying away and the carting. The stringing had been done by men in the spring and had nothing to do with the hand-picking casuals. They worked on stilts – ten to twelve feet high. I never worked on stilts. I think too much of my neck! I mean those chaps could run on them and they weren't short stilts.

The farm started moving about half past five or six in the morning. Basically the hoppers were up in the hop gardens and standing by their baskets by seven o'clock. As long as somebody was there to hold the basket it didn't matter if others joined in later on, such as children and other relatives. There were different modes of picking the hops. In mid-Kent they picked in bins. In East Kent right round our Faversham area they picked in baskets.

The system was in the old days when the hops were grown on poles that they had a pole-puller, bin man and a tallyman. The pole-puller pulled the hops down so the women could pick the hops off, and [the] bin man, he stood there and helped the cart to pick up the hops. He opened the poles to shoot the tallies of hops in and the tallyman used to go in and measure them up and that was all put down in the modern days by a book and a pencil. But in the early days the tallyman had a special system for tallying hops. Every picker had a stick with a certain number on it and they used to file a notch on for a certain number of tallies. So the old tallyman used to go round with a series of sticks hanging round him. It was accurate. Of course it was all done by book and pencil when I was at the farm. Some of the pickers were a slippery lot: they'd try and get the hops in twice for measuring up if they could. So it was a job where the tallyman had to have his wits about him. He'd go to each family in turn and when their baskets had all been measured up and marked down then the cart came along with the tallyman and as they measured the hops they chucked them up on the cart.

When they got a load they'd go along to the oast where the hops would be dried. This was a highly skilled job and the hardest part of it. The drying was done with oil-fired burners in the kilns at the top. The heat goes in at the bottom, up through the hops and out at the top, and that's how they're dried. The hops are also flavoured with sulphur to keep them the right colour and make them right for the beer and the brewing.

The hoppers never worked Sundays – that was sacrilege. As far as Saturday working was concerned if it was a big crop of hops we used to try and get a turn-out till twelve o'clock. So they worked from 7 to 12. Saturday morning working was going out fast because basically the hop pickers weren't as poverty-stricken when I was managing as they were in the early '20s and '30s when they were more or less forced to work at the weekend. Originally it was six shillings for a tally (a blooming great thing in size) and six bushels to the tally. Some of the women could do, if they were good that is, two or three tallies a day. It might not have been a fortune but it added to the family income. They never had any money when they'd finished. They used to draw the money and they'd blow it before they went back, most of them. They really came hop-picking to get clothes for the kids before the winter but half the time they used to blow it on booze and that's how the old hop-picking job went on.

About ten o' clock was what we used to call 'Beaver Time' when they had a bit of grub and it would tide them through till dinner time at twelve o'clock when the bin man would blow a whistle. They didn't necessarily have to stop and some of them picked right through. They finished at five o'clock at night so about four or half past four the bin man would blow the whistle and yell out 'Pull no more bines!' and whatever part of the pole they were on would have to be picked and stripped off ready for measuring up.

They ate in the huts or at the tables on the heath. There was always plenty of bread, 'tatoes, and plenty of eggs. They used to have big frying pans you could do about twenty or thirty eggs in. Of course they'd get out and get fish and chips and bring that in in the evening and the weekend when they had a few bob to come. They'd always draw up to two-thirds of their money on what they picked unless they were finishing up in which case they'd draw the whole lot. So usually it was near the weekend when they'd start to buy a bit. Fried stuff was the basic. Stuff it in the old frying pan and fry it up! It has a taste all of its own – a bit of bacon, sausages, plenty of fried bread. Eggs. When I was a boy sixty years ago I remember going to Penshurst to my Aunt Lu's when she was out picking at Penshurst. I'll always remember the eggs. She had a blooming great frying pan then and she had about two dozen eggs in the pan and those eggs tasted beautiful.

As far as the fires were concerned we used to supply the hoppers with free faggots and cork wood (a thicker wood). Of course the governor used to moan and said they had too many big fires at night when they had the old camp fires going in front of the huts. They had all sorts of old gear for the fire – dixies, buckets and so on. They used to make themselves an iron-frame fire with a few bricks round it and they'd soon get the water hot for a cup of tea. Of course people were used to electric kettles and all sorts of things in the '50s. In fact they used to put so many electric gadgets on they used to blow the fuses out in the farm. It was my job to see that they didn't do this because it was an absolute nightmare. Just as you were settling down about eight or nine o'clock thinking everything was done, hoppers would come banging at the door saying, 'Oh the lights have gone.' They'd fused them because of all the toasters and warmers and heaters and God knows what and then it used to be a right old picnic and you'd have to read the Riot Act to them and tell them what they should and shouldn't do – not that it made much difference, they still done it. They weren't supposed to have anything in the huts because there was always a great danger of fires in the huts. There was a terrible fire fifty or sixty years ago when all the huts burnt down. All went up in flames. You can imagine – they were all wooden huts except the roofs so once they got going in the wind it went straight through them like a bush fire.

As far as toilets were concerned in the '50s the toilets were chemical ones. They had these chemical buckets and stand-up toilets with a corrugated iron roof and a door – primitive affairs. Obviously before that they had never even had that. Washing facilities. Well there was always a water cart pulled out in the middle of the square in front of the hoppers' huts – a big water cart that they could draw water from. Plus the fact that there would be stand pipes at each end of the camp for boiling water. So there was no problem about water.

They used to call it 'The Heath' in front of our hoppers' huts and they used to hang out their washing there. Some of them didn't do a lot – in fact some of them were a bit grubby, I tell you. But they did a bit of washing on a weekend. Friends and relatives used to come down from London and The Heath used to be filled up with cars – sixty or seventy cars on The Heath. They used to get together Saturday nights and Sunday nights and have a right old booze-up. The pubs used to be full up and the hoppers rolling about and the kids hanging about outside, some of them crying and some scrapping, and the others inside getting drunk and singing. They had a good time. They liked a drink. Some of the men used to slip off at dinnertime to the pubs for a beer. We didn't look on it too well.

Basically they tried to get the kids to stay in the hop gardens and help them pick, but knowing what kids are they never did. The kids tended to get away and get into various bits of mischief and pinch a few apples, but basically they weren't too bad. They were kept pretty well under control.

The mission hadn't gone by the '50s. We had a mission hut which was kept 'specially for the missionaries who helped look after the pickers. They used to hold little services up there Sunday mornings. It weren't all that well attended but the mission was very good. They did a terrific amount for the hop pickers, looking after their little bits and pieces that went wrong like septic fingers and rashes and cuts and bruises – all the sort of things you get in a hop garden. The old mission lady – she was a lovely old lady – she'd been away all over the place even out in India – she was very strong with these hop pickers. The mission was based in South East London – Southwark. You can imagine the amount of poverty in that area after the war. They used to have a surgery and the hoppers would stand at the mission door. Actually she was a very, very good doctor. She did me a good turn. I wasn't all that well and I went to see her and she looked at me and gave me an examination and said 'I want you to go to Canterbury Hospital and I want you to go there *today*.' And she gave me a letter and she phoned up the hospital and the result was I had major surgery. I always reckon the old girl in the mission done me a good turn. She was a very astute and clever lady and did well for those hop pickers.

Some of the women was pregnant when they arrived. Before we knew where we were we were having to get the doctor out or they'd have a miscarriage or something, but they didn't seem to mind. They used to love coming out hop-picking. Friday nights they'd be up the pub singing 'Hopping Down in Kent'. They'd do a bit of dancing, and the old mouth organs got going. People used to get tossed up in the hop pocket when people got excited. We didn't have a hopping supper, but we used to have a rare old time when hopping was over.

Our hops went to the Borough of London. Today most of it goes to Paddock Wood. Then the London Borough used to be the special market and the governors (that is the people who run the farm) and the managers (like me) used to go up to the Borough to have a look at the hops, see what they were like and then we got – drunk.

Now I worked for a family company that had been hop growers for about five hundred years. My governor's father was a major and his father was a 'Sir'. Now they do say that the old grandfather had a problem about what they were going to pay the pickers. The pickers had a strike. And the grandfather went up the hop gardens and said 'Don't stop but I'm not going to pay you any more.'

Now that night they reckon the pickers went up to the big house and they collared the old chap and they put a rope under his arms and they dropped him down in the well and held him just above the water. And they said 'If you don't give us any more money on these hops we'll drop you down the water, and he said he wouldn't so they dropped him in the water. When they pulled him out the second time he said he'd give them the extra money. So they evidently got round their little problems by that method. I don't know how true that is but that's what they say happened.

H.E. Bates (1905–1974)

From *The Blossoming World* (1971)

Many of H.E. Bates' novels have been televised and the character of Pop Larkin (who finds Kent 'just perfick') is a comic and endearing one.

The Blossoming World is the second of Bates's three volumes of autobiography. In it he deals with that period of his life when he moved to Kent with his wife Madge and it will be a surprise to his Kentish readers that he initially found the 'natives' 'a withdrawn, dark, ungiving people, insular, defensive, highly suspicious of strangers, distrustful of all intruders, hard to make friends with'. Their great 'festival' hop picking, however, intrigued and delighted him and he saw it as a kind of pagan religious rite, in which all participated.

From *The Blossoming World*:

And then while the chestnut was still being felled and split, the first actual work in the hop-gardens began: that beautifully fascinating business of stringing the poles so that the whole garden takes on the look of some gigantic white-gold spider-web. Then soon came the white of pear and apple blossom, the even whiter bloom of cherry, and then last the pinks and reds of apple. In mid-summer hay turners, still horse-drawn, rattled about the meadows and in August binders, horse-drawn too, clacked about the fields of oats and wheat and barley. By the time plums had grown purple-fat on trees and had been gathered by the real festival of the year, the English *vendage*, the hop picking, began, bringing the centuries-old fusion of Cockneys from London and the people of Kent, in almost precisely the way peasants forgather for grape-harvests in autumn in European vineyards.

I always felt that this festival, for which surely every working family turned out, was not only gay, as indeed it was with all the chaff and joking old-buck backchat and teasing and beery fighting and wenching that went on in and around it, was something more than just the mere business of picking hops for brewers; it always struck me as being a sort of pagan rite. And thus, I always felt, the people of Kent perhaps also saw it, though not of course consciously; it was a rite that had to be attended, a festival that had to be worshipped at. Nobody, except toffs and squires, ever missed hop picking. Every mother took every child with her to the hop-gardens and every child, except those still being suckled at the breast, picked hops, from the first dewy misty light of September mornings until the soft descent of dusk and its shouted evening benediction that rang out down the pale-green lines of fallen or half fallen hop-skeins. 'Pull no more bine!'

They pull the bine by machine today and every year the Cockneys come in smaller and smaller numbers. There are things called quotas and you see somewhere every year the saddest of sights that can surely blight a fertile country: whole gardens of hops being burnt as they stand.

Bob Kenward

Songs About Hop-Picking

Bob is a well known and popular songwriter of Kent, whose tunes have been sung across the county by many singers. A former organiser of the Tonbridge Folk Club among others, Bob is a regular performer at folk clubs and festivals across the South-East and has appeared on television and local radio. His CDs, The Man of Kent *and* The Straggling Bine *are still available and Bob's contact details are on the Tonbridge Folk Club website. Most recently he has written and performed* The Rise of Captain Swing, *a folk drama in song with the Kent Song Collective.*

'King Hop' or 'Hop is King' (1980)

This fine poem to music personifies the hop and traces progress through the calendar year and on to a resurrection after death (harvesting), much in the way of the many John Barleycorn folk songs. Bob points out that biologically this should really be 'Queen Hop'!

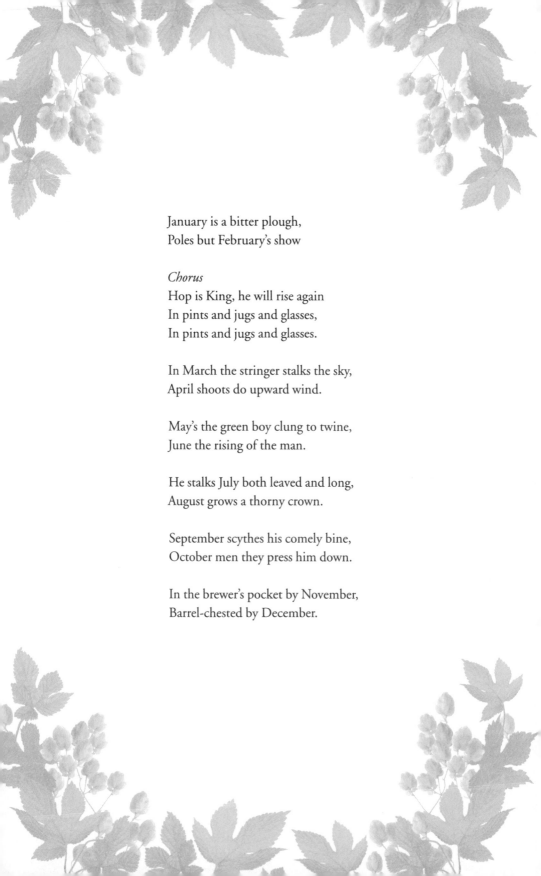

January is a bitter plough,
Poles but February's show

Chorus
Hop is King, he will rise again
In pints and jugs and glasses,
In pints and jugs and glasses.

In March the stringer stalks the sky,
April shoots do upward wind.

May's the green boy clung to twine,
June the rising of the man.

He stalks July both leaved and long,
August grows a thorny crown.

September scythes his comely bine,
October men they press him down.

In the brewer's pocket by November,
Barrel-chested by December.

'The Straggling Bine'

This combines hop picking with another great passion of Bob's and inspiration for his song writing, the railways and the disappearing Kent stations formerly used by the London hop pickers. Interesting social observations include the Sunday visits of 'Dad', who goes home drunk having spent some of the family earnings on beer.

The hoptime comes and we must go
On the Southern line;
Crammed in a carriage away from the Smoke
And how the sun do shine.
Paddock Wood we sit and stare,
Horsmonden we're almost there,
How we sniff at the country air
And the Straggling Bine.

It's off at Goudhurst by the mill,
On the Southern line;
Half a mile to climb the hill
And how the sun do shine.
To the hut and through the door,
Drop your suitcase on the floor,
Just like home to see once more
The Straggling Bine.

The pull-and-push runs like a clock
On the Southern line,
Telling us that it's time for work
And how the sun do shine.
Out into the gardens green,
Pick a bushel and keep it clean,
As many leaves in as can't be seen,
From the Straggling Bine.

Sundays Dad comes for a spin
On the Southern line;
He goes home as tight as sin
And how the sun do shine.

We work among the gardens here,
Where sky is blue and air is clear,
To make his pot of docker's beer
From the Straggling Bine.

Every morning brings the goods
On the Southern line;
Struggling through the fields and woods,
How the sun do shine.
Every kid from London Town
Loves to run these gardens round,
Hiding where he can't be found
In the Straggling Bine.

It's pockets packed and carried in trucks
On the Southern line.
Scrub in a bucket and brush yourself up
And how the sun do shine.
Sing and sup the Hopper's Toast,
Kiss the one you love the most,
Say ta-ta to the Farmer's Oast
And the Straggling Bine.

It's down to the mill, we'll all go home
On the Southern line;
Cots and prams and kettles and stoves
And how the sun do shine.
Horsmonden, Paddock Wood,
Back to the Smoke and the neighbourhood;
Dad says the air must have done you good
In the Straggling Bine.

'The Lesson of Hopyards'

This song is closely adapted from Thomas Tusser's Five Hundred Points of Husbandrie, *with an added chorus. It is on Bob's* Man of Kent *CD, where it is accompanied by 'Pickham triple-tracked harmonica' and has been featured by the brewers Shepherd Neame for their hop-blessing ceremony.*

Whom fancy persuadeth amongst other crops
To save for his spending sufficient of hops,
Must willingly follow, of choices to choose,
Such lessons well-learned as skilful do use.

Chorus
New hop for old
Farmer prove bold,
For the Lessons of Hopyards
Is Hop is worth gold.

Ground gravelly, stony or mingled with clay
Is naughty for hops any manner of way,
And if it be mix-ed with rubble or stone,
For dryness and barrenness, leave it alone.

Choose soil for the hop of the rottenest mould,
Well dung-ed and wrought, as a garden-plot should;
Not far from the water, but not over-flown.
These lessons well learned are meet to be known.

The sun in the South, or else Southly and West,
Brings joy to the hop as a welcome-ed guest.
But wind in the North or else Northly and East,
To the hop is as ill as a fray in a feast.

Meet plot for a hop-yard once found as I've told
Make thereof account as of jewel of gold.
So dig it and leave it the sun for to burn,
And afterwards fence it to serve for that turn.

The hop for its pocket I thus do exalt;
It strengtheneth beer and it flavours the malt.
And being well brewed, long kept it will last,
And drawing abide, if ye draw not so fast.

Chapter Six

The Continuing Hop

John Lander (Hop Consultant)

Hops – Past, Present & Future (1992 & 2013)

John Lander has had a lifetime's experience in the hop industry as grower, marketer and consultant. He lived for many years in a converted oast house in the village of Offham in the centre of what was once an important hop-growing area in mid-Kent and he now lives in West Malling, not far from the fine belt of former hop-growing land in the Medway valley described by William Cobbett. This article was originally written in 1992, just before John retired as a hop consultant and he has added a 2013 'Postscript' to bring it up to date.

In the article John sums up the story of hop-growing in England from its growth in the sixteenth century to its present smaller size and suggests that there may be bright prospects for the industry in the future, albeit in a changed form. The cultivation of the hop, however, can no longer be concerned with the harvest workforce and the seasonal 'invasion' of Kent by East Enders and Gypsies. The introduction of new strains of miniature hops, mechanically harvested, marks the end of an era – the closing chapter in the social and agricultural history of the hop.

❦

There are watersheds in most enterprises and there are many examples of peaks and troughs in the history of hop growing in England. The 'hopping' of beer began in the sixteenth century following the introduction of hop cultivation into this country by Flemish settlers. Keeping qualities, commercial production of hops expanded to reach its peak in the late eighteen hundreds when almost 72,000 acres were being grown. At that time, every town of any consequence had its own local brewery and demand for hops was at an all-time high.

Production of hops during the First World War was strictly controlled and, apart from a brief period afterwards, disaster hit English hop growing in the late nineteen-twenties when many growers were unable to sell their hops due to a collapse in prices brought about by surplus production. This dire situation was saved in 1932 by the creation of the Hops Marketing Board, a statutory body established under the Agricultural Marketing Acts. All growers were required to market their hops through the Board who regulated supply with demand by establishing a quota system for each farm. Over production was eliminated, prices recovered and prosperity returned to hop growing once again. This happy situation lasted for 50 years and probably saved English hop growing from extinction.

This newfound prosperity enabled many new techniques to be introduced, particularly in the nineteen fifties and sixties, as well funded research into chemicals, spraying methods, engineering and plant breeding meant that crops were no longer decimated by pests and disease. But the biggest transformation of all was the move from hand to machine picking. The familiar sight of thousands of hop pickers descending on the English countryside in September has now disappeared for ever. Wye College's plant breeding programme not only saved those growers whose hops had to be destroyed as a result of verticillium wilt by producing varieties which were tolerant of this killer disease, but they also produced new varieties with much improved brewing values. This period, too, could also be described as one of the 'peaks' soon to be followed by yet another unforeseen 'trough'.

The advent of the Common Market brought about the demise of the Hops Marketing Board in 1982 as a compulsory marketing organisation as such bodies are contrary to the Treaty of Rome. In its place six voluntary co-operative marketing groups emerged, English Hops Ltd, the direct successor to the Hops Marketing Board, being the largest.

One of the failings of the compulsory marketing system was that, although it managed the internal UK market very well, it was completely hamstrung when it came to exports. The English Hop Industry was totally unprepared to meet the challenge of world competition whereas the Germans, Americans, Czechs and others had long experienced these tough trading conditions. Many English growers found that they were unable to continue growing hops profitably at the prices dictated by world market conditions and gave up. More recently prices have improved somewhat and there has been financial support from the E.E.C. in the form of an annual acreage payment to supplement the lower prices achieved and a once for all payment to assist growers to grub unwanted varieties and to plant those which are more acceptable to the brewer. However, the future is still uncertain. Most years there is a world over-supply of hops; beer consumption in the UK remains static despite excellent summers and the world market remains very competitive.

Despite tough trading conditions, there is the prospect of another advance in the techniques of growing, processing and marketing which could become another watershed in the history of hop growing. Wye College has just released, for field trials, new varieties of 'super' hops which could give English growers the edge over their foreign competitors. An even more dramatic change could be the move to 'dwarf' hop growing which would change the face of the countryside from the now familiar tall wirework to 'hedgerows' of hops no more than 8 feet high. These would be picked by mobile machines which would straddle the rows. Given the provision of sufficient capital, this dramatic change could proceed apace with many consequent savings in growing costs. There is, too, an increasing move to market hops in extract form rather than in the traditional form of dried hop cones. Not only is the latter very bulky to transport and store, but the brewing value deteriorates rapidly within months whereas extract in its liquid bottled form is cheap to store and its shelf life is almost indefinite. A company at Paddock Wood are now offering many forms of processed hops on a worldwide basis.

With a new generation of hop growers emerging, and given that sufficient energy, determination and capital is available, there is no reason why English hop growing should not succeed again and achieve fresh peaks in years to come.

Postscript (October 2013)

Unfortunately, my 1992 prediction of better times for English hop growers has not happened. Worldwide competition on prices remains intense. However, a small group of English growers who are highly efficient and very mechanised survive, many of them growing new varieties of hops which find a ready market. It is difficult to forecast what the future holds. Wine drinking has had an impact on beer consumption. There has been a big increase in local mini brewing, but their total consumption of hops is limited.

Gael Nash

Living on a Hop Farm (2013)

Gael was born in Scotland and moved to south London at the age of 5. Gael taught in Guildford and Dulwich and married a barrister, who later became a judge. Gael achieved academic qualifications in sociology and comparative literature and is a published poet. She has lived for the past twenty years in a converted granary on a farm once much involved in hop production.

❧❦❦

Living on a Hop Farm

Some years ago, my husband and I moved from South London to Kent and for the past twenty years have been living on a farm in East Sussex. Many farmers have in recent years converted farm buildings into private properties. We viewed the four conversions here when they were finished. There are two converted oast conversions and an attached Wagon Lodge. Our house is a detached granary, which was originally the tractor shed. We are situated round the farm pond which has been here since the eighteenth century, when the farmhouse was built. The pond was used in earlier days for the cows to drink from. We were not a listed property on completion but the law changed in 1998 when all buildings within the cartilage of a listed building were automatically included. Restricting, but accepted by us!

Living on a farm and being primarily town dwellers, we trod carefully. The farm was mainly dairy but had several hop gardens on site and several acres around the area and the farmer's family have a long history of several generations in farming. Our farmer died about ten years ago and his son has taken over but his wife still deals with all the farm's finances. He is buried in the bluebell woods within the farm, taken up to his grave by tractor – his love and his life. We miss his courtesy, friendship and acceptance of us.

My memories of those early years are the smells and sight of the hop gardens and as I look across to our paddock, I note the progress of a single hop we were given by the farmer in memory of a member of our family who would fly over the farm regularly in his plane – an 'Islander' – and would swoop low over the hop gardens to make his presence known.

Life has changed, farming has changed, and there are now only four hop gardens remaining 'on site'. The fields are now growing a different crop, mainly rape.

The Oasts Gate, Court Farm, Northiam. (Oliver Nash)

The smell these produce is much more invasive, penetrating the atmosphere and not as pleasant as the original inhabitants of that soil! The fields across from us to Bodiam are strident yellow in colour.

Choices and tastes have changed. Of the 46,000 acres of hops that originally flourished in the county locally, only 1,000 survive and the migration of hop pickers from London is no longer needed. In the years we have been living here, there have only been transient workers, mainly from the Continent. There are still the remains of where hop pickers stayed. This was mainly in a large barn where the farmer dried the hops after picking. Originally they were hung in the roundels of the two oasts which have been converted into dwellings.

We decided against buying one of these because of the height of each roundel and therefore the cost of heating bills! As an addendum – there was the question of furnishing circular rooms.

We are situated in an idyllic setting. At the bottom of our garden runs the Kent and East Sussex Railway which runs from Tenterden in Kent to Robertsbridge in East Sussex and stops within walking distance of Bodiam Castle, that stretch now having been restored. We can also walk along the banks of the River Rother to Bodiam. The railway was used for the filming of George Orwell's book *Animal Farm*. We hear, see and smell the steam that exudes from each passing train. The line is set considerably lower than the fields so the view when travelling aboard opens out the adjoining farmland.

Charles Dickens was a regular traveller on this line and wrote, 'The hop gardens turn gracefully towards me, presenting regular avenues of hops in rapid flight, then whirl away.' What a picture, what a memory, but now, sadly, no longer. The criss-cross scaffolding of hop poles and wires that were visible in the past are now limited, but the farm on which we live grows enough hops to supply their own beer. This is brewed on the farm here and sold locally as 'Level Best'.

When our farmer was still living he produced two new varieties of hops which still exist. Barley is grown locally for local beer and the brother of our deceased farmer is now growing two local species of dwarf hops. Real ale is popular so new varieties are welcome.

The memory I have of entering the barn where the hops were drying was the pungent smell. This smell varied from year to year. The farmer gave us dried hops to hang in the house and some to plant outside our back door. Unfortunately, it gave rise to asthma attacks. I was never asthmatic, living in town, but my 'peak flow' was affected by the prevailing winds which blew across the fields and to our garden, filling my lungs. Gone, therefore, is my romantic dream of a hop-filled decorative interior to our home! The sensation of the sharp leaves causes a reaction to my skin. However, there are many compensations for the life we have here. The open countryside, the sound of the dairy, the love that small children have of running through the paddock and their attempt to count the number of rabbits that burrow and dig potentially dangerous holes in the garden and eat most of the plants we endeavour to grow!

The romance of hop has never disappeared. Growing them has always been a challenge and no two years are the same. The farm still carries the smell in the air and the history is absorbed by all who visit. When we see and hear the wind blowing through the cowls of the oast houses across the pond the history of the hop farms and the hop pickers of old come to mind and the smell in the air floods the imagination. Although it has become much cheaper to grow smaller hop vines in Belgium and to produce cheaper beer, there is fresh hope for young growers who are now reviving old hop gardens and producing smaller microbreweries for smaller markets and pubs.

There is a revival of hop festivals which is helping to make English hops almost fashionable again. Even as Londoners we need to encourage them to show that we do belong here and to pass on their heritage to the next generation. We owe them homage for their history.

Also from The History Press

KENT

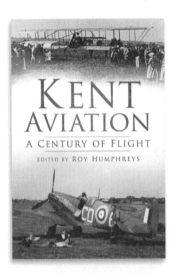

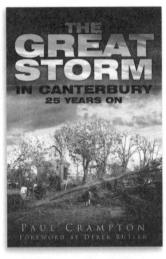

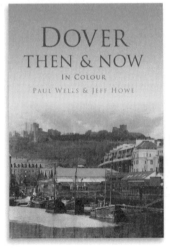

Find these titles and more at

www.thehistorypress.co.uk